This story is dedicated to

Gill, my sister,

Who was there at the start of the journey,

And

To Simon, my husband,

Who will be there at its end.

"Oh, I am fortune's fool!"

William Shakespeare, *'Romeo and Juliet'*.

"But, he thought, I keep them with precision. Only I have no luck anymore. But who knows? Maybe today. Every day is a new day. It is better to be lucky. But I would rather be exact. Then when luck comes you are ready."

Ernest Hemingway, *'The Old Man and the Sea'*.

"Are you what is called a lucky man? Well, you are sad every day. Each day has its great grief or its little care. Yesterday you were trembling for the health of one who is dear to you, today you fear for your own; tomorrow it will be an anxiety about money, the next day the slanders of a calumniator, the day after the misfortune of a friend; then the weather, then something broken or lost, then a pleasure for which you are reproached by your conscience or your vertebral column; another time, the course of public affairs. Not to mention heartaches. And so on. One cloud is dissipated, another gathers. Hardly one day in a hundred of unbroken joy and sunshine. And you are of that small number who are lucky!"

Victor Hugo, *'Les Misérables'*.

"You own everything that happened to you.

Tell your stories.

If people wanted you to write warmly about them,

they should've behaved better."

Anne Lamott.

Mr. Lucky!

Mr. Lucky? Is that a good title, a good reflection of what is contained herein? I think so, though it might not appear so at times.

This is my autobiography, my life thus far…..

There's lots of swearing and shagging to keep you entertained, lots of sorrow – no 'memoir' would be complete without yer actual sorrow….but my life has been pretty funny too so I have included some stuff to make you smile.

Everything here is the truth, the whole truth and nothing but the truth. Or at least as far as I remember it. Half a century – a lot to remember! Some things – tunes, places, voices and conversations are all so clear in my mind even now, easy to recall, yet I can't remember my mobile number half the time!

All the people are real, everything described, happened.

All seen from my point of view.

I want to leave something – I can't paint, draw, write novels, invent stuff so this will have to suffice. Maybe it will end up on someone's bookshelf, passed around to friends – in that case, I WILL have left something and that will suffice. It will be good to know as I am scattered – in the land that, in my heart I never left, in all my wanderings: Kernow, back to the wild, wild sea.

Enjoy.

MUM: Sorry for swearing. No Celestial Golden Ear Whizzes, please.

CHAPTER ONE.

FINGS AIN'T WOT THEY USED TO BE…..

In which our hero returns to the land of the Gods, becomes bamboozled and then finds himself a SGWM (GSOH, DDF) who would like a LTR. (Someone who isn't a tosser would be good).

'Crash'.

By The Primitives. No.15. April 1988.

"Please…just **SHUT UP**. I've had enough……"

~ ~ ~

M4.

M5

A30….

We arrive at our new house. It was late. SO late. The van barely made it up the incline to the car park, but after what seemed like days of travelling we were there. Brand new life. Me, John, Snowy, Sooty, Prince, Lena, Sam and Freddie. Everyone pissed off, tired, needing a wee. All of us.

"Ooooh! I need a slash," said John. *"Like, **now**. The animals will too,"* and with that he opened the door and the dogs, startled awake, all jumped out and

started weeing like it was the finals of The Great Weeing Competition. Up against car tyres and in people's front gardens.

There was a gap in the hedge so we two went through it and wee'd, in the only way you can when you've been sitting for hours and hours then you stand and gravity takes over and there is nothing you can do to prevent the weight of liquid seeking its escape. So we wee'd, and wee'd, John me, while the dogs ran round like things possessed, and when we'd finished, we went back to the open van and found the cats had gone. Fer fuck's SAKE!!! We'd only been here five minutes……

"SNOOOOOOWY! SOOOOOOOTY!!!" bellowed John, who had gone from blissful to ballistic in the blink of a zip. *"WHERE ARE YOOOOOO?"*

"SHHHHHH! Shut up! You'll have the neighbours on at us. It's nearly midnight."

"I DON'T FUCKING CARE. I'VE LOST MY CATS!!!!. THE NEIGHBOURS CAN GO AND FUCK THEMSELVES. SNOOOOOOOOWY!! SOOOOOOOTY!!! COME ON!! WHERE ARE YOOOOOO?" and with that he took off, over the hedge, through the trees in the pitch black. All I could hear was snapping of branches and OW! and OUCH! FUCK! and OW! MY FUCKIN FACE! as he plunged like a madman through the trees.

Lights began appearing at windows, in our little *cul – de – sac*. Not a propitious start for the two poofs and their menagerie…..

"Can I help?" said someone.

"Oh, no, its OK. We've just arrived and lost the cats. My…er friend is trying to find them."

"FUCKING CUNTING CATS!" bellowed John as he appeared over the hedge, bloodied and scratched in the dim lights from people's windows.

"Ah John. This is one of our new neighbours. Mrs…..?"

"Val. You can call me Val." (Fag hag. That's a good sign).

"Ok, er..Val, Sorry to have disturbed you. John's just worried about his two…."

…cats, which were sitting by the front wheels of the van, looking completely unperturbed by all the noise.

"They're there, John. Look. By the van…"

John ran down the grass to the van, yelling SNOOOOWY!!! SOOOOTY! and the cats, understandably alarmed, legged it. Oh god no….

"COME BACK!!!! COME BACK!!! SNOOOOOWY PUSS PUSS PUSS!!! SOOOOOOTY!! COME ON HERE!! HERE!!! PUSSS PUSS..

"They're not going to come back with you yelling at them. Just leave them they'll be back. Shut up fer Chrisssakes. Its past midnight…….Val, I'm so sorry…"

*"No, Really. It's fine. It's been……interesting"….*as in: it'll be all round the neighbourhood before dawn that two poofs are moving to no.64….

We'd had the foresight to put a mattress and some sheets on the van last. So, after pacifying John, who was by now practically sobbing, we dragged the mattress out and across the grass, possibly smearing it in dogshit, but I was past caring, and in to the house. No64. My very own house.

We dragged it in to the lounge and then John disappeared and came back with the dogs, who were bounding around like mad things and Freddy, who by this time had decided it was *'QUITE NICE!'* again and kept saying so.

Freddy shouting, John snoring, the dogs pacing and whining – I think I just cried myself to sleep.

Dear reader, as you can probably guess, this was doomed to failure and it wasn't long until the cracks became far too wide for any roll of wallpaper ever made to cover; they became fissures that were never going to close. It was OK for the rest of the Easter holidays, before I started my new job (EEEEEK!) as we had domestic 'challenges' to overcome , such as how to stop the cats pissing off every time we managed to cajole them in to coming into the house. They were probably quite happy – liberated from the concrete suburbs that was Walfamstowe into the stretches of Arcadia that was The Beacon. Why WOULD they come in? They were out! They were doing cat stuff, and were not about to regress….we rarely saw them over those following three months until in the end, they never came back at all. John had moved by then so they had probably found a more peaceful solution. Decisions to be made over where to put the furniture, where the dogs were going to sleep ("NOT IN THE FUCKING BEDROOM!! NO NO NO!!!"), what John was going to do with himself now – not much chance of a job really, given his 'problem', although he did actually, after he'd moved out, get a little job in a Nursery, doing God knows what, or even how. He hated it of course, and began to stop off in the pub on the way home – they had lent him a little van to transport the plants and stuff around, and so luckily we both had transport but it did mean I couldn't keep my eye on him - and I only say this from the point of view that it was ME who got the shitty end of the stick if he'd been to the pub on the way home as I'd get in to find him either asleep and the hall swimming in dog wee because he hadn't taken them out, OR just shouty and aggressive, full of blame and spite because I had *MADE* him come to this fucking place where there aren't any fucking street lights (of course there are, you silly man) and where, apparently *'nobody fucking talks properly'*….. Out of the two, I preferred the first, dog wee notwithstanding – that was moppable - I could get out in the clear air with the dogs and he'd leave me alone.

A very weird thing happened, dear reader, which I want to include as it just demonstrates what it was like dealing with my Dad. Cast your mind back a few chapters, to 'ARGHHHHHMYSONSAFUCKINHOMOGATE'. Cast out, abused by letter, shunned, and rejected….not a good time for me. Then six weeks of obsequious gratitude and living in his house with conversation restricted like we were in Stalinist Russia or something. In the end, after I'd moved, I had, of course to tell them about John. I rang one day and whilst on the phone, John yelled at one of the dogs or something, and Mum said, "*Who's that?*" and I grabbing the bull by its bollocks, decided to confide in her.

"Oh. That's john. He, um, lives here. He's erm….my…my friend. I mean boyfriend…" (he was 20 years my senior – 'boyfriend' seemed a bit stupid. 'Sugar Daddy' wasn't appropriate, as he had no sugar. Daddy then? OMG. A pattern emerging and I didn't even see it!!)

Anyway, to the phone call.

"Yes, my new…erm partner. Well, not that new actually. We've been together for a while. He's……"

"Freddy, shut the FUCK UP!! I'll shove your beak up your fucking arse if you don't stop yelling….!! came John's dulcet tones from the kitchen.

"Oh. He sounds quite um…loud," said Mum.

"He's a Londoner," was all I could think of to say.

After a few strained pleasantries, during which time we didn't speak of the huge John shaped elephant in the room, we hung up.

Half an hour later, - and I have absolutely NO IDEA what went on in that room after our call – the phone rang again.

"It's your Mother. Your Father says to bring your Friend over for tea and biscuits this afternoon. Bye." Hung up.

To say I felt surprised, is somewhat of an understatement. Head fuck! WHAT game was he playing now? But I decided we'd go. Why? Don't know. Because my Dad said so, and so I had to do it? Because I was too shocked to refuse? Because I wanted to see what would unfold? Or was it because I'd hoped there was forgiveness, reconciliation between a homophobic Father and his son? The last seemed the least likely, the most bizarre, but the option I preferred.

"John. We're going to Truro this afternoon. OK?"

"'Spose so. What for?"

"Because my Father has invited us for tea and biscuits." Even as I said it, it sounded completely unreal – I had long since given up such imaginings.

"Oh. OK," was the reply. Is that IT? **'OK'?**

So off we went, John – I kid you not – in a suit and tie, despite my protestations – to towards Truro and who knew what.

The IDEA of it, as it turned out, was nowhere NEAR as surreal as the actual event…..

We rang the bell, John and I, and waited on the doorstep – the Devil Spawned son and his equally perverted fudge-packing friend – and my terrified Mother opened the door – grey faced, impassive apart from the eyes which darted wildly to the person behind me, checking he wasn't in drag or wearing slap (this, from the woman who gave it some welly in the gay bars of Brighton…), decided it was relatively safe, remembered to say hello to me and stood aside.

We walked in.

There he sat, my old man. In his chair, King of all he surveyed.

"Em..this is John. My….uh……well, John. John, this is my Dad."

"Hello, Sir", said John. (Brownie point, x10). *"Pleasure to meet you. Nigel talks a lot about you."* (Nothing you'd want to hear however). And they shook hands.

"Get the teapot, Darl," he said. Teapot? TEAPOT?? *"Sit down, please."* This was getting to be a like a meeting of civil servants, in the 40s. Totally doing my head in….

Mum went out to the kitchen. I followed…

"What the f…… heck is going ON????"

"I don't know. He just said to ring you. Now you're here and I really really don't know what to do…."

"Well, it seems to be OK. What the hell is he playing at?"

"I have no idea". She looked beaten. Scared.

"Look, it'll be OK. Listen…."

And there they were, homo and homophobe, the abomination and the perfect, yakking away like old mates, like they'd known each other for years.

"Trevor, we need some more sugar. We'll just nip down Spar, OK?"

No answer. Too busy talking.

We went out, glad to be out of the tension. We were AGES! When we got back, they weren't there, but we could hear voices. Looking out of the French doors, we could see down into the garden and they were, tea and fags, guffawing and hooting with glee. This was just too much. It was like a parallel universe where my Dad was a nice guy and didn't want me dead after all! There he was, talking to my lover like he was his best buddy. Super weird. The only explanation I came up with was that because John was an older man, he had somehow disassociated himself from his obsession with our bedroom activities, forgot that this man whose fags he was nicking was NOT the same person who, in his fevered imagination stuck his cock up his son's arse. Whatever the reason and however this insane meeting came about, I couldn't fathom but, as we watched them I couldn't shake the feeling that something ghastly was going to happen. My Mum rested her hand on mine on the railing, both looking for and giving comfort.

"Oh there you are! Where's the bleddy tea? We're CHACKIN 'ere!"

"Sorry, yes. Just coming!" said my Mother / servant and hurried off to make a fresh pot which we drank in the garden, eating custard creams in the sun at Uplands Crescent. The afternoon passed in a haze of tension and well, confusion and when all the tea was drunk and the biscuits eaten, he just stood up and said,

"Well, nice to meet you. Bye"

and went back into the house leaving us just sitting there. I was anxious not to leave Mum with whatever aftermath there may be but even more anxious for this whole charade to be over, so I stood too, said, *"Right, we'll be off too then, bye Mum. I'll ring you,"* and dragged a confused John out of the back gate, shouting *"BYE DAD!"* but not looking back.

That was the first, and last, time they met.

One of the weirdest days of my life.

So, we returned home where he immediately reverted to who was becoming an increasingly aggressive and angry man. And hit the bottle, several door frames and the bed.

As you can imagine, this whole edifice was ripe for collapse. He didn't like Cornwall, or the house, or the job, or the accent (Please…..) or probably even me by now. I didn't like him, him being in my house, him getting pissed and screaming at me, chucking things around, ripping the leg of the bureau (*"Its MINE"" I'll do what I fuckin want wiv it….."*), breaking the glass in the cupboard in the sideboard…….not really conducive to harmony in the home, eh?

We used to fuck still but it was cold, mechanical, passionless, and usually only on Sundays after a session down at the Borough; he'd be pissed and 'manly' and insist on his 'congergals', as he called it, never having seen the word. So off we'd traipse up to the bedroom, he'd strip off, make himself hard, not noticing for one second that I was somewhat reluctant, as evidenced by the lack of interest in the nether regions….still, I'd lie down, put up with the perfunctory fiddling, try to make him come, to get it over with so he'd then sleep it off. But, this day, he decided he wanted a fuck. A proper fuck.

"But, John I don't really want to. I'm not in the mood…."

"You're never in the fuckin mood. My cock not good enough for you? Too big is it?"

"No, John, of course not. It's just you're a bit drunk and you always get a bit rough and you hurt me when you…."

"Well, I'll do it gentle then. You used to like it rough. What about that night back in Selina's with the butter?" (I fancied you then, you moron).

"I know but it isn't really very….."

"OH WELL, JUST FUCK OFF THEN! YOU ONLY WANT SEX ON SUNDAYS WHEN YOU'RE PISSED (Which part of that are you not surprised about, John?). *JUST FUCKIN FORGET IT. I'LL HAVE A WANK. AS USUAL".*

"Stop yelling at me! Look I'll do that if you'd like me to…."

And I went to get hold of his erection, still really hard, fuelled by his anger no doubt and started to wank him off, but he just knocked my hand away and stormed out of the room.

"I'm going to have a drink," and he went, stark bollock naked down the stairs, his cock bobbing, leading the way, spluttering with temper. This was not looking good.

I gave him a few minutes, hoping he might just go to sleep. I went down shortly after to find him in the lounge, sprawled naked in the chair, masturbating furiously.

"SEE? I DON'T FUCKIN NEED YOU…." And he shot his load on the settee, and his legs. *"HA!. THERE!! I'M STILL A FUCKING MAN. I CAN MAKE SPUNK. NOT LIKE YOU, YOU FUCKING QUEER. ALL YOU DO IS..IS…..WHERE'S THE BRANDY? WHERE FUCKING IS IT?"*

Brandy and John were a spectacularly incendiary combination; it was what fuelled the violence between him and Carlos, and I did my best to keep him and it apart. But, not today. Naked, cock wilting and covered in his own semen, he lurched in to the kitchen, and got the (full) bottle from the cupboard. I *was* fucked, but not in a good way.

"I DON'T FUCKIN NEED YOU. I CAN HAVE SEX WITH ANYBODY. ANYBODY. EVEN ME!!" and he started pulling on his dick again….

*"ANYBODY WOULD WANT THIS. MY COCK IS MY PASSPORT TO EVERYWHERE. EVERYONE WANTS IT. 'CEPT YOU. YOU'RE A FUCKING MISERALE CUNT AND I DON'T KNOW WHY I'M HERE. TOMORROW I'M MOVING OUT. WIV ALL ME ANIMALS. OK? **OK?**"*

He looked so pathetic, naked, cock now soft and floppy, leaning on the door jamb or else he'd fall over (how the hell did he get so pissed? We'd only been to the pub and I was with him…) but although he was slowing and slurring, I was still in jeopardy.

"AND YOU. YOU FUCKIN LITTLE POOF. I'M NOT QUEER. NOT LIKE YOU. YOU PANSY. FUCKIN POOFTER….."

What? I was being abused by a man who had just tried to stick his cock up my arse for being gay? This was now getting surreal…

"John, listen…."

"I'M HAVIN A FUCKIN DRINK. YOU CAN PISS OFF IF YOU DON'T LIKE IT." And he started drinking brandy. From the bottle. This was not going to end well.

"John, look. I know this has been difficult for you. This transition. But it will get…", I started, pointlessly to say but was cut short as he hurled the bottle of brandy at me. It was a very poor aim, missed by miles but hit the reinforced glass window that Council houses all had at the time, the sort with a wire mesh in and smashed. Shards of flying glass, animals bolting for cover, brandy splattering everywhere, over the furniture, the walls, the carpets and me. And that, dear John, was the Rubicon and you just crossed it. He lurched to his feet and went to the hall where he slithered down the wall, beneath the portrait of his Mother, and started his usual routine of *"WAHAHAAAA I'm sorry Mum. I wish I was dead. Why did you leave me blah blah….* He was slumped now naked and sad in the hallway and I, fearing for another assault, though in reality, he was done, stepped over him and headed for the door.

The End.

The next morning, as usual, he was 'really really sorry', and it 'wasn't really his fault' (I thought I'd let that one pass) and 'it won't happen again' (that one too) but I too had made a decision, so, sitting on the chair nearest the (open) back door, I said,

"Look I thought about what you said, and I agree. I think it would be a good thing to do."

"What?"

"You know, what you suggested. Yesterday......"

"Oh, I was a drunk. You know. I didn't mean it."

"Oh."

"What did I say?"

The bit about moving out. With the animals."

"I never. Did I? Well, if I did, I never meant it."

"Well the thing is. John. I think it'd be a good idea. So I was thinking, if we went to look for a bigger place, for you to rent for a bit – you'd get your rent paid cos you're on the dole – and then when you're settled, I could come and live there and we could rent this house out and make some money ....so let's go down town and have a look in the window. What do you think?"

I'd made this last part up. No fucking way.

"Hmmm. Yeah, ok. Sounds good. I hate this fuckin' gaff anyway. And that nosy old bitch over the other side. Come on then..."

So that's what we did, and, as if by some miracle, there was a house, sent by the Housing Angels, way WAAAY on the other side of town (in Love Lane, ironically), vacant, available, willing to take pets and ready. RIGHT NOW. Fan-fuckin-tastic.

Comment [nb]:

Within two days, he was gone, all the animals and their stink, Freddie and his incessant yelling, poor Sam (who I would miss terribly but it was a good trade, if you ask me), all the ghastly furniture and the threat of violence. All gone. And…..breathe. Breathe in the clean and empty air.

I did used to go and see him (and, my bad, make him have sex – his cock and hairy chest were still a pull, even though *HE* was a wanker, and I could go home after. Shameless. Don't care!) and to take my darling boy out for long walks – he of course, along with poor old Prince and Lena were left all day as he was still working at the nursery. The cats (which miraculously had returned) were OK, because he cut a hole in the back door….

I don't know how long this went on for – a few weeks, I think, but he suddenly announced he was going back to London, to live with Joe. Joe, his ex, with whom he had a relationship even more violent than the one he had with Carlos. To his small flat. Where they got streetlights. And they spoke propah. So he did. Packed up. Drove off. Gone. I only saw him once more…..

…..months later, I had a call from him (still alive then. Didn't know about Joe…) asking if I would be willing to take Sam back. The flat (DUH) was too small for him and he was working (as a hearse driver!! Just perfect!) and had no time to exercise him plus Joe didn't want him there and he smelled (Sam that is) and he was too big and it was Joe's flat etc etc….Yes, John, I will. End of.

So we drove up to Gordano Services on the M5 near Bristol and he drove down from London with Sam. The poor dog got out the van, and he could barely walk. I was horrified. He was about twice as fat as when he'd left and his nails were so long he couldn't walk properly. He saw me and hobbled over and just stood, silently, head down, before me, in recognition but also fear – fear maybe that I wouldn't take him. All anthropomorphising, I know, but there was no question. I walked over to John, this man, the man I allowed to make love to me, to do the most intimate things and I looked at him and all I felt was……nothing. Just nothing.

"Thankyou. He'll be fine now."

Sam got into the back of the car (much to Lisa's chagrin) and we drove off, back down the motorway...

M4, A30 Home.

Sam was home too.

CHAPTER TWO.

BACK ON THE BIKE.

In which our hero finds himself lost, found and lost again. Then found again.

'The Only Way Is Up.'

by Yazz. No.10, July 24, 1988.

It just HAD to get better, surely? The only way is UP now.

~ ~ ~

Fuck, fuck, fucketty fuck.

It was all very well, but I was now living on my own. For the first time. EVER. And I hated it. John had (thankfully) taken most of the furniture, but his presence still lingered, like a particularly malodourous fart; the kind he used to do in fact. What I needed was a Good Spring Clean. And some more furniture, obviously. I was working of course, and earning, so for once I had a proper amount of money which was not allocated for Beer Money, as it had been in the past: do some work, buy beer. Do some work, go up the pub. Do some work, go Up West, with Chris and get involved in some hare-brained and properly unfortunate set of circumstances. No I was a House Owner. I was a Pillar of Society. I would buy…..a Settee! Who'd have thought, eh? Anyway, in the event, I bought two pale green velour Chesterfields. (Gimmee a break! It WAS the mid-80s!) and very nice they looked too.

Went to work, watched telly, went to bed, went to work, went to the pub, went to bed…..this wasn't how it was supposed to be. Need a man. Need some how's yer father….this was long before YouTube and Xtube. Masturbation, whilst OK for the time it took, is a solitary pursuit. I was sorely lacking in the real thing. So I decided, weekend, I'd go to town and…er..see. 'The Hole in the Wall'. That's where I'll go. No, not what you're thinking, although given that happened later and the fact they're practically adjoining, they could just make a hole….save time, see?

The Hole In The Wall.

It's an old debtor's prison, now a lovely pub and this is where I headed. Why? No idea. It was very nice, very noisy, very drinky, but I felt…well, alone. Nobody knew me, nobody spoke more than *'Right?"* and *'Right, are ee?"* and then went back to their beer. I had a couple of pints, couldn't find the loo (it was actually outside.) so I decided to head off back up through town to another pub, to see what was what. I don't know what I expected to find, really - a friendly face would be nice. I got half way across the car park and realised I hadn't done a wee. There was a public toilets in the corner and that's where I went. The two urinals were flooded so I went into a cubicle. I sat down. I was a bit pissed and a more than a bit pissed off. Fed up. Tired.

Cornish Country Cottage....

Then. The foot appeared under the wall. Yes, dear reader, I had apparently chosen the local cottage for a wee and was being *cottaged*. For the second time in my life. Not quite as posh as Harrods, but nevertheless, the chance of a bit of cock was undeniable. Any gay man reading this will know, will understand the pull of such an opportunity. And I took it. I nudged his foot back. His hand appeared then, waving in the air, presumably expecting me to put my cock in it. As I was still sitting, fully clothed in the toilet, this wasn't really a practical proposition. Remember, I was quite unused to this (honestly) and there appeared to be a whole set of rules and codes that I knew nothing about. So, I kind of tickled his palm. I *know*. But I didn't know what else to do. It was a bit *'round and round the garden'* which, unknown to me, was a signal for the next stage. Or maybe he was just making it up, but the next thing, his lower half – his legs (no trousers or pants), and his cock and balls appeared on MY SIDE OF THE WALL! Two things went through my mind, completely unconnected to each other and the possible danger of this situation. One was......Mmmmm what a beautiful cock, fat and lovely hairy balls and wanting to touch it and suck it and do what any gay man would do presented with such a treat, and two.....fuck! This is really dangerous.....what if we're caught? How would he get out in time? He was naked and had half his body stuck under the cubicle wall. And certainly I was party to such shenanigans..... *"Oooh, no guv. I was just having a rest and these legs and genitals just APPEARED! I had no idea what was happening…"*. I'd heard a story once about a bloke sticking his todger through a glory hole and the bloke the other side STUCK A HAT PIN RIGHT THROUGH IT! Think about that for a minute…..

Then, as if on cue, diminishing any chance of the erection I had begun to develop, some people came in. Well.., men. Hopefully they'd see the piss-filled urinals and leave. But, what if *THEY* were here to do a bit of cottaging and found the two cubicles locked, and decided to look under the door?

"This is where poofs come for shagging, you know," said a voice.

I froze.

"What, in 'ere? Why?"

"I dunno. There id'n nowhere else in town to go I 'spose."

"Never knew that, Bri. What do they do?"

"Oh just give each other blow jobs. They stick their dicks through a hole in the cubicle walls."

"Really? How do you know that, Bri?"

"Oh. I just do, tha's all. Bleddy disgustin', if you ask me. 'Tid'n right. Blokes together. Queers, 'n that….."

Silently as a panther, a very scared panther, I had taken the only course of action I could think of and was crouched up on the toilet, so my feet weren't showing. Meanwhile, matey was still under the wall, cock wilted, bollocks shrunk up in fear, no longer so attractive, actually. Frozen, not moving a muscle, presumably able to see the feet of the people who were possibly going to murder him….don't look under the door, boys. Please. Just go…..

"Bleddy hell I need a piss. C'mon. Fuck, look at that. The bogs're blocked. Fuckin disgustin'.

Then someone, presumably 'Bri,' rattled the door of the cubicle.

"Bollocks. Engaged."

Then I heard him rattle next door.

*Bleddy 'ell, tha's engaged too. (*pleasegopleasegopleasegodon'tlookunder…*)
We'll have to do it outside.*

"Yeah, but Bri. How do you <u>know</u>? About queers 'n that?"

"Just fuckin shut up. C'mon."

And they left, to pee up the wall outside and then on to the next pub. Much relieved, I got down off the toilet and my 'friend' began to extract himself from under the wall. I was just waiting, trying to still my racing heart, when a note came under the wall, written on bog roll, in biro (it must be a Thing – Bodmin, Harrods – all the same in the search for cock) which said: 'TOILIT, LANIVET CAR PARK.TEN MINITS'.(it must be a thing to misspell, too). The toilet flushed, the door unlocked, and he was gone. Obviously I didn't go. I was on foot and anyway, no matter how delicious had been that set of genitals, I was really shaken up by what had just happened, and aware to the potential danger had been in. Thinking back on what I'd heard, it seemed to me that 'Bri' knew far too much about the 'mechanics' to be that unversed or inexperienced himself. *'The lady doth protest too much, methinks….'*

Anyway, a bit drunk, a bit cold and now, in spite of a near brush with being murdered and dismembered and making all the papers, and now a bit randy (even NOW), I got a cab to the top of town and went in to The Garland Ox, just for 'one for the M11' – Rodney, you will ALWAYS be a bad influence, wherever you are now! – and stood at the curve of the bar. And bam. Pulled Just like that. Bit skinhead – y, but definitely up for it. Hurrah for beer goggles! We did the old *'looking, but not looking'* bollocks (do you ever wonder how much time gets wasted, in the world's bars, by this petty rigmarole? *You* want to. *I* want to. Why are we doing this? Maybe a safety device – if you're wrong, you can just pretend you *weren't* ogling, you just happened to be glancing in that direction. 47 times.), then he came over and said: *"Wanna drink?"* and I said, *"I'll have a lager."* (brief flash of Chris's grinning face, watching me heading for catastrophe, with foresight of angels). Ah well, at least it was something I could talk about over (select) dinner tables) and he said, *"I ain't seen you in here before."* And I said, *"No, I haven't' been here before. Just moved here."* And he said, *"Oh. Wanna drink?"* and I said, *"I haven't finished this one yet"*, and he said, *"Well, drink up then",* and I said, *OK, I'll have a lager"* and he said, *"OK... Nigel"*

WHAT?? How could he know me??

"My name's Nigel."

"Oh, so's mine".

"Mustve meant to meet then. Wanna a drink?"

"No, really. I can't drink that fast, I've still got the other one."

"OK. I'll just have one before we go."

'Before we go'? Excuse me? But then he scratched his crotch and that was that. Fortunately he only lived down the road, as I was now severely incapacitated – Chris would've been ashamed. Fuckin lightweight! – but, though I'd had about six pints, my beer goggles were well and truly in working order.

We got to his place, went straight up the bedroom, he stripped, started to take my clothes off and…..

This time, gentle reader, I cannot tell you more. Not because I fear for your sensibilities, but because I barely remember any of it. Was probably good, but I can't be sure. I remember he was hairy (tick), nice cock (tick) and he was a good kisser (tick) but what we DID…….well….

I DO remember though he was into being spanked. HARD. I, undressed, but not very able, managed to make him come, eventually. There was some CBT (look it up!) I know that and a lot of shouting and him calling me 'Master' and 'Sir', but I have no idea what I actually got out of it. He came, I went. Never met him again, though I lived in the town for another seventeen years. Actually, I *did*, briefly, but in a very different set of circumstances….

The following morning, with a banging headache, I decided that being a SGWM (GSOH, DDF) was a bit rubbish. I hated being on my own and then as if the angels were listening, I had a call from Gill. She and the Hairdresser (that she'd left London for) had split up. *"Never mind!"* I said, sympathetically. *"Come and live with me!"*

And so it came to pass. Again.

SO, here we were, the blackest sheeps you could imagine, back together. I suspect this was thought to be a very good idea by Pater as Gill was bound to keep me on the straight (no pun intended) and narrow, but as you can imagine it was anything but. Gill copped off fairly soon after with a bloke from the pub. It was bottoms up! In a 2CV. Use your imaginations people. It was fairly successful until one morning, after I had negotiated the pants hanging from the antlers of the large stuffed stag's head that John hadn't taken and was still over the stairs, reminding me daily, and I went to the front window to find the said 2CV had rolled down the car park, over the embankment, across the road and down the embankment the other side and was now resting, nose first, against the wall of the flats opposite. With all its lights smashed. Oh dear….I yelled up:

"TOM!!!! (Let's call him that, for privacy's sake, if you get my meaning). *"Your car's rolled away. It's across the road…"*

"OH FUCK! FUCKKITY FUCK!! How the hell will I explain this?? What happened?"

"I'm guessing you left the brake off?"

"What can I do? Gill. GILL!!! What can I do?"

I have no memory of what the solution actually was. The result was we saw Tom a little less often…

Sis and I were often down the pub. We were both working, and we had (for the first time in my life) quite a good disposable income and we had fun for those few months, through that summer. My GSOH returned and it felt good to be able to make it up a bit to her after the debacle of Forest Gate. How would it have been if the thing with John wasn't happening? Would she have stayed, or gone regardless? I think it was just jolly bad timing...

..but now, it was like we were making up for it. We were kind to each other and were enjoying each other's company. She, of course, was entirely *au fait* with my past – indeed had been a favourite at the Court of Rodney, back in the day, and so we had plenty of shared memories and 'do you remember's to keep us going.

Something worth recounting here as it chimes with a later event, where all harm is undone and I was able to see things more clearly; the longings for and unfinished pathways of pain still being trodden, is an episode when Gill and I decided to go up to London to see Rod (me) and Kath (her. And me). We got on a coach and went back to Ilford, the scene of my burn out, where all my hopes and dreams were tattered and scattered in my bed along with tissues and the semen stains of other men.

Why, you may ask, dear reader, do you want to revisit this...this....agony? Answer: *'Cos I luv 'im'*? Um....no. *'Because I* **loved** *'im'*. Past tense. At least that was what I was telling myself.

Anyway, off we went, back to the big new gaff, up Ilford Lane, where by now (don't ask) Rod was back living with Kath in a bleddy great house, big enough to have converted the cellar into a bar.

We rang the bell, two small people, nervous orphans, returning, hoping for.....what? For Gill, I guess another dollop of the unconditional love they always gave her, and me....some absolution, some resolution of what had happened to my perfect life. And probably a final shag. And as we expected (hoped) even after an absence of several years, arms and heart were opened and we were welcomed in.

Much hilarity ensued down in the bar, which after cuddles and whoops of joy, was the first place we went, to drink toasts to the past, to homecomings, to old friends, to family – so many toasts, we were fairly quickly wazzed.

So, we all sat and laughed and remembered, and Rod was sitting on the old settee and I anxiously went to sit with him; he put his arm around my neck and pulled me in, and said, *"Nige. So lovely to see you, babe"*, and I was undone. In that moment all was forgiven as I inhaled him and breathed out the hurts of the past we'd shared. Did he know? Was he feeling the same? It was all too late now – we were living in different universes (though probably, if he'd asked, at that moment, I would have crossed them and gone back – to what? Disaster, of course) and too much damage had been done. But for that moment, when he enfolded me, took me home, in his arms, the world was whole and I was filled with perfect grace and light.

Inevitably we went upstairs, and there he was – brown, hairy, erect and willing and we made love so slowly, so tenderly – like the world stopped, we two were the only living souls, in communion. How could something so perfect, so sacred have become so sullied, so broken?

After we had come, and lay in the silence, I asked. I asked the question that I'd held for the longest poisonous time.

"Rod?"

"Hmmm. Yes babe?"

"Why did you, you know…. do it?"

"What?"

"The thing with Kenny. Why did you chose to be with him, like you did, with me in our house, having to see, hear, smell the two of you? I'm not asking for apologies – it was what it was and is long past *(Clearly, it wasn't…) just an* explanation"

"I don't want to talk about it, Nige."

"I do, though"

He sat up, all the evidence of what had just happened glistening in the beautiful trail of belly hair, and said,

"I need a shower".

I followed him in.

"Please Rod. I have to know it wasn't me – that I wasn't inadequate, second best…"

He turned, cupping his balls in a strange attitude, suddenly looking crumpled and vulnerable, resembling St. Sebastien, and said,

"Nige, you were NEVER second best. You were the love of my life. I fucked up."

The whole world hung in the silence that followed that sentence. What? Then….

"I loved you more than I could ever say. You know I'm bad with words 'n that. But you brought Kenny back to the flat and I heard you and it really hurt me and I wanted revenge 'cos I felt betrayed, you going with somebody else (Excuse me??) *so I just wanted to hurt you for a bit and then Kenny got serious and I was stuck and then you met Ken and you was gone and it was too late and then Kenny fucked off, but you were happy with Ken..*

…..he was sobbing now, years of pent up confession…

…*but I thought I could get you back but it wasn't the same when you moved in so I thought you'd be better off with him so I made you leave again. It was all fucked up and I never meant it. You were the love of my life and I fucked it all up. If only you hadn't…..*

"Whoa, hang on….you can't blame all that on me. And anyway, I didn't do anything. He left. Oh Rod, what fools we were."

"Yeah, Not many, eh? Still, we're back together now, eh? You could move in. Kaff'd love it and......"

What did he mean? Was he saying.....?

*"It would be the same thing, Rod. Your heart may be mine but your cock, your body will never be and I won't settle for less. We'll end up the same. So, no. I can't. But you have no idea how much it means that you asked. You were the love of **my** life too, you baldy ole bastard"* and with that, the world returned to normal and it was done. The reason for this visit had, for me at least, become clear and I knew now we were cleansed. It *WASN'T* me, he *DID* love me and he really had been sorry. As sorry as me and that was enough. We had become each other's favourite memory and it was good.

Time passed, the weekend flew and we left, Gill and I, and I didn't see him again for twenty five years.

Autumn was approaching and in September, I once again met up with Steve.....I had decided to try to find him and had tracked him down through his surname and, thinking that as he was down in the South West somewhere (and Dorset wasn't that far), and I soon would be, it might be nice to meet and mend our differences, or at the very least have a shag. 'For old Time's Sake', as it were. As it turned out, we did both. To my surprise, it turned out that he was living only about ten minutes away – with his new boyfriend – well not actually *THAT* new; they'd been together for some time, not that that made any difference – so we arranged to meet up. He was renovating an old stone barn (on his own – no mean feat) and when I drove up, he was there, glistening, muddy, glorious. Was this a good idea or a bad one? I was ONLY meeting up, to catch up, for old time's sake as I said. But, fuck me, he was beautiful. My memory and mind were racing.....could we? Were we alone? Is this a good idea? There's always consequences, you daft old tart....

"Hi", he said.

"Hi!" I said. *"How are you? You look well"*. (*WELL*? Somewhat of an understatement).

Two 'Hi's' and a half naked man.

"I'm fine. Long time, eh? What – eight years? Are you OK? Where's that fuckin Chris? He's not with you is he?"

"Yep. Eight years. (*Eight years* since I fucked you, and you fucked off). *I'm fine. No, he isn't. He's dead."*

"Oh, fuck. Really? Look, I'm sorry. I know he was your mate (you have NO idea). *What happened?"*

"AIDS."

"Oh."

A four month silence followed. You never were very big on difficult stuff like *Emotions,* were you?

"Yeah, well. Doesn't matter now. A year now. Nearly. Miss him though. Anyway. Came to see you, not to moan about stuff. Doing a grand job here…."

"Oh, yes," he said, grateful to be let of the petard he had hoisted himself on. *It'll be great when it's done. If it ever is….,* he laughed. "Well. Come on in. His Majesty's at work. He won't be home for hours yet. Plenty of time…."

'Time'? Time for what? Though I knew perfectly well…..a gin and tonic or four later, my at-risk driving licence far less of a concern than what I knew lay between those thighs, thighs even stronger than when last I saw them…

"I need a shower. Been digging for hours. Hot work…" and he started upstairs. Then looked back, and like a whore, I followed, not being able to stop what was now clearly going to happen; nor did I want it to.

He stripped off his work clothes, and there he was. Bronzed, more muscular, as utterly beautiful as I remember. Thick black chest hair, that impossible trail of belly hair, the riot of dark pubes in which nestled his astonishing cock. Hooded, but beginning to stir. I was, once more, helpless and hopeless to resist, not that I could've or would've - only the arrival of His Majesty was going to prevent this.

"Shower?"

"Yes. Oh yes!" and I undressed too, never looking away from that gaze that he'd lazered me with, so long long ago, and walked across the room, in to the wet room and into the arms of the man who had both broken my heart and brought me the fiercest joy of my first love; who had lifted me to ecstasy and brought me to despair; who had shown me the physical joys of who I really was whilst all the time was with another. The agony and the ecstasy. Yet here we were, wet and hard against each other; all that fell away and we moved to the bed, not bothering to dry where we fell into each other's souls and body. He still fitted me like a perfect skin, no pain, even in our haste just that long burning headlong slide into bliss.

I recount this, so many years later and see it clearly but am wise enough now to understand that that was just how *I* was feeling; to him, it may just have been a fuck, a *cinque à sept,* a quickie when the chance was there. I didn't care then and I don't care now. It DID flicker through my fevered dopamine filled brain at the time, but so fucking what?? For me, it was thrilling, passionate, a <u>*mémoire*</u>, a reminder of what I had spent so many lost and painful years searching for – a man, not this one of course; too much history, too much pain, but a beautiful man who filled both my spirit and fantasies, making me feel *whole*. Just for a moment.

After (too, too soon), covered in our sweat and semen, we showered again, smiled shyly, dressed and returned to our flat gin and tonics. I had gone before His Majesty returned and we never spoke of it again.

Some weeks later, Steve phoned.

"There's a party on, down west. We're going. Wanna lift?"

"Nah. I think I'll stay here thanks." The last thing I felt like was getting all ponced up, and going to a party with a load of people I didn't know, pretending to be having a good time, a sort of New Year's Eve enforced jollity.

"Please yer fuckin self. Stay there and be miserable then. C'mon. There might be some spare cock."

"Thanks for that". My SGWM status had become particularly boring now; the GSOH had evaporated. Vicious circle really. Who wants to be around a misery ass like me?

Then, as if on cue, I heard his voice: *"Fucking hell, you're a miserable cunt. No wonder you haven't got a boyfriend……"* and he was right. Again. Chris, I love you and hate you, both at the same time.

"No, actually, Steve. I will. Give me half an hour I'll drive over to yours, OK?"

"Well I wasn't thinking of picking you up, you twat. You're 30 miles in the wrong direction. And back, and then again if you don't pull. See you in a bit."

I raced upstairs, chucked on what was lying around (no time for prettifying these days), got in the car and drove to Steve's.

"You going dressed like that? Bloody Hell. Not like when I knew you before. Quite the dandy gay boy then, with your big gay hair….."

"Yeah, well that was the 80s. It was allowed." (Embarrassing memories……moving on….). *Anyway, it's only a party. It'll do. What's wrong with jeans and T- shirt?"*

"It's **OCTOBER***…….never mind. Come on, let's go I have to set up before it starts."*

To my relief, as it would have been a tad embarrassing, having shagged the last time I saw him, to have His Majesty with us. He wasn't coming, so it was just me and Steve. Also embarrassing, given the noise and wailing of our last encounter. However, it wasn't mentioned and we drove down in companionable silence, only talking when fond memories arose – and there were some, to be resurrected from that bloody time.

We arrived, and it was in a cow shed, the party, or a barn, full of hay bales like a hoe-down and the smell of cow shit. And lesbians. Loads of lesbians. It turns out that the hosts of said party are brothers, both gay, with a gay sister. Ooof. Well done, Mum and Dad. She had obviously invited every lesbian in Cornwall and far too early...Steve hadn't set up his 'Diamond Vision' screen yet; that's why we had to be there early. I wandered around the loft, with a beer, like a turd in a swimming pool. My mind went back to that night, long ago, in 'Brief Encounter' and my experience of being 'in the wrong tribe'. Obviously, I wasn't going to fit in to the lesbian's 'division'.

I thought back to my night, with Rod in Gateway, on the King's Road in London, the notorious LESBIAN ONLY club in the West End, and the longest running lesbian club in history. They filmed parts of 'The Killing of Sister George' in it you know.

Beryl Reid and Susannah York, 'The Killing of Sister George'.

Begun in the 20s, it survived all through the war and beyond, fiercely protective of its heritage and clientele. How the hell Rod managed to get us in I have no idea but I can quite honestly say it was one of the most terrifying nights of my life.....these women were *seriously* butch: short cropped, slicked back hair, drawn on moustaches and 3 piece suits, with dainty pretty little girls on their arms. I clung to Rod like a frightened limpet, praying that no one would speak to me....he, of course charmed the erm..dungarees off 'em. It didn't make sense to me, but it was no different I guess than the red-hanky wearing, fist fucking denim boys in the Colherne or the L.A., or the tee – shirt tied twinky boys in

Brief Encounter. I think what didn't make sense then, or indeed now, is why we can't all just get on? Why do we all have to be exclusive? Like we don't have enough trouble? Those drag queens didn't get the shit beaten out of them in the Stonewall to create this segregated, gay – within- gay world, surely? I'm just an idealist I suppose – I'm not saying that like doesn't attract like, that the hairy blokes like other hairy blokes and that CDs shouldn't have their own places of sanctuary, but really…this fenced in attitude, not approving of twinks in a bear bar, or a lesbian in the LA. Seemed wrong. Still does. To me, anyway.

These Cornish dykes seemed harmless enough, even if a bit dismissive of a strange (as in 'unknown') homo wandering around the edge of the room with a beer, wishing Steve would fucking hurry up so I would have someone to talk to…..my attempts at conversation had mostly been met by grunts of acknowledgment – not hostile exactly, but not inviting me to have a conversation. I had another beer and waited some more. The room slowly began to fill. Another bloody group! Homos from down West, who all knew each other. I circulated some more, wearing a groove in the straw on the floor. I had another beer as I passed the table. It was going to be a long night. *'Dallas'* was on. I should've stayed home and watched Crystal and Alexis bitch slappin' and brawlin' and the *'Golden Girls'*.

Unknown to me, whilst I HAD been at home, moaning to Steve about how pissed off I was and how I didn't want to go to the stupid party, there was another man who the weekend before had been dumped by his lover of ten years (standing, not age) who had come home from work and said *'I'm leaving. Bye!'* leaving a devastated and bewildered man behind. That same man had been bullied into 'getting out', and 'getting over it' by his mates, thrown (literally) in to the bath and practically frog marched to the party, where he Would. Enjoy. Himself.

I heard them come in. Heads turned, appraisals were made, crotches were examined. Three or four of them, I don't remember now, but one was particularly striking He had a sadness clinging to him and my mothering instinct lit up. Awww, bless, he need cheering up…. Actually, he was quite attractive in a 'beary' kind of way. A little overweight. No, solid. That's more accurate. Very short hair, beard. Quite sexy really, especially with these beer goggles on. He too, was scanning the room, checking out the possibilities. Just habit. He might've had a broken heart but there might still be a cock or two, eh? I was looking at the new group, all of whom knew everyone else – much MWAHing and hugging while looking over shoulders at who else might be around and available – and he, scanning, came to rest on me. Stopped. Our eyes met. And moved on.

The party grew, the noise got louder, the voices shriller, the snogging more ardent, the camping more theatrical and the bitching more exquisite. He was looking over again. So, obviously, was I or I wouldn't have known. By now, I was sitting on a hay bale, having been propositioned by what I thought was going to be a top shag, but in spite of all the leather, turned out to be like Kenneth Williams when he opened his mouth.

"Oooh, hello love! Hiyaaaa! How are you? I've been vardering you all night. I quite liked 'er over there, but 'er riah's all a bit too zshooshed up for me. I like my omis butch. She's a bit omi-polone for me. You gotta a bona eek though. Nice riah too, if you don't mind me saying. I hope you don't mind me saying, do you girl? I always say what's on me mind, and when I saw you trollin' round the gaff, I thought 'Ooooh! She's got a dolly ole eek, I'm going to HAVE to open me screech and say hello. I 'ope you don't think I'm too forward?'

If ever this was a mismatch this was it – head to toe in black leather, wrist cuffs, peaked cap and camp as the campest thing in the Campest Man in the World Contest. I was kind of flattered – but not in any way tempted. It was like being in an episode of *'Round the Horne'*. I briefly tried to imagine what sex with him would be like. Hilarious I imagine. Like trying to shag John Inman.

"No, I don't mind, but……."

"Mike. Piss off, eh?" said a voice, and there was Mr. Bear, coming to my rescue! He moved away again, after Mike had gone off in search of someone more sympathetic, after the kind of glance that said…well you know. Just milliseconds too long, weighted with intent. He went back to his mates and I sat again on a bale. I looked over. He was looking too. Oh myyy.....

We spent the next half an hour edging ever closer along the line of bales along the back wall of the barn. Edging. Pause. Edge. Pause. Then we were on adjacent bales, only separated by some orange binder twine. Then a hand laid down on the straw, then mine just next to it. A hair's width between. Heart beating. Waiting. Then. A brush against my little finger, and our hands rested side by side. Another weird cottagey sort of this but without the smell of urine. Breathe…. Then his hand on top of mine, holding it loosely, loose enough in case I wanted to pull away. And in that moment began the next nineteen years of my life.

"David."

"Erm… Hi. Nigel."

"We're going to get out of here for a bit now. It's too noisy," and he just led me out. I found this exciting, but was the first of a million times he would control what I did. But of course I didn't know that then. A bit pissed, magnetically attracted to this older man, signals reaching my groin now. We went to the tractor shed and fell into each other's arms, kissing hard and desperately (he, I guess needing reassurance after what 'that cunt Steve' had done) and me…well, just wanting sex with this man.

He pushed me down, so that I was kneeling. And stood over me looking down and I could see him hard in his trousers. (Trousers, not jeans! This is relevant.)

"What would you say if I went down on you?" I breathed. Yes, dear reader, I REALLY did say that! How ridiculous!

"Try. Find out," he said. So I did. I got his cock out and sucked him off in the tractor shed. Classy bird, me.

Steve came out and went over to his car, which was parked next to the shed. Banging on the roof, he yelled:

"OI! YOU TWO! If you get spunk on my car seats, I'm sending you the bill." while we watched, giggling, hands over our mouth from the darkness of the shed.

"Can we go back to yours?" he said.

"Not sure. I didn't know where Gill and her 2CV man were. *"Steve. STEVE! Can we come back to yours tonight?"*

"No worries. Leave the key out. I'm staying on 'cos I need all my stuff."

So we drove away, away to bed, to beautiful sex with this wonderful hairy man.

This was the first night of the nineteen years I was with him.

October 22nd. 1988.

CHAPTER THREE

EXIT, PURSUED BY A BEAR.

In which our hero loses his shape, get chipped away and made into a facsimile.

'One Moment In Time'.

by Whitney Houston. No.1 October 1988.

You know that moment, everything seems to come together? We did.

~ ~ ~

It was going swimmingly. I thought this was IT. I was in LURRRVE with this big hairy man, and he with me. He lived 'down West' with his wonderful black lab, Lisa, in a lovely Cornish stone cottage. I lived in a terraced ex-council house on an Estate, with plasterboard walls and really REALLY weird neighbours. What to do? We just couldn't live apart – I was driving 30 miles after work to his place, and 30 miles back the next morning, all sexed out, books unmarked, lesson plans rehashed….staying down there weekends. Poor Gill – pretty much deserted (Again. Men eh?) though this did mean the house was empty for whatever shenanigans she got up to. Many I hope, though she's never said…..

As I said, it was all going well. Apart from the fact that Mr Bear hated Gill. He was at first polite and friendly, and we all got on 'fine'. Me, ever the dork, saw nothing wrong. I was living with the two people I loved most and we had FUN! We went to the pub together, did stuff…but I was unaware of the seething resentment building….nothing specific, nothing overt…

It was New Year, 1988 and we were due to go to the pub with two lesbians we'd got very friendly with, one of whom, coincidentally Gill had once worked with (and was terrified of) years before. We'd been up on the Beacon with Lisa and Sam (who was by now, acclimatised, slim and the most loving creature I have ever known. He was also a TOTAL wuss – afraid of leaves, children, the wind if it made his ears flap) and the two women came towards us and their black standard poodle came running over. Lisa was delighted and showed him her Bally; Sam hid behind my legs, peering out like ScoobieDoo. We passed, nodded, said *'Hello, oooh what a nice dog',* etc and went our ways.

The conversation WE had, as we walked away, was apparently identical to the one they had: *"Gay". "Yep, deffo." "Tell a mile off." "Yep."*

We met them again the next day, in November of '88, stopped, chatted and became the firmest of friends for the next 19 years. Until I left, that is, but that's a story for later.

We were all there, that New Year – the 'Girls' as we called them, though Jean was 20 years my senior and Mary 15 – their kids, and what a swell party it was. At midnight, if you did a conga, they'd give the leader a bottle of Champagne (well, probably Asti Spumanti or similar. Who cared?? It was freeee!) as the conga went past the bar. So we just kept changing leaders until we had a bottle for each of us, about 15 all lined up on the table. Which we drank. Somehow, drunk as the proverbial skunks, we ended up back at someone's house, drinking whisky out of priceless china cups, and I managed to persuade the daughter of whoever's house it was that I was actually, in real life, Miss Budapest, 1956. The fact I was British, male and it was the year I was born all seemed to escape her. She marvelled and insisted on sitting next to me – maybe she thought she was in with a chance, me in me white suit 'n all. Ha! Wrong tree. Anyway, even drunker, David decided it was time to go; he was probably right (before I trashed the heirloom) but I, as drunks always do, insisted on one for the road (M11?) and thus began a little friction as Gill sided with me. I was too pissed to notice the resentment in his face and of course I agreed with HER. The evening ended being poured into a taxi and then…….no idea.

New Year's Day, après party. 1989.

There were no rows that I remember, just a gradual wearing down of her spirit. Then sadly one day she announced she was moving out, to share with a friend as it was 'nearer work' and so once more, we parted, not happily, but of course, I had mah man, and as usual that was all that mattered. I know she will read this and in my defence I will say that I had no choice – he was implacable, immovable and very very cunning. I am sorry, Sis – I should have been bigger, stronger but he was stronger than me. Clearly he wasn't willing to share my affection or attentions; she *apparently 'made me stupid and childish'*. I thought she made me laugh and be child*like* – there's a difference – but what he said, went. And therefore, so did she. Not too far away and we saw each other often but there was always a massive elephant in the room or the car or the pub and it was wearisome. And sad. She never knew why he disliked her so intensely and neither did I, but……Sorry Gill. Really, I am.

So the next thing, David moved in, got rid of all my furniture, brought his, and so my 'married life' began. I only needed .4 of another child and I would be Nuclear! And so went the next 14 years.

Get a promotion	√
Go to parties	√
Go out to Dinner	√
Go to the theatre	√
Go to work	√
Go to friends for dinner	√
Go to Friends for Christmas	√
Have friends over for dinner	√
Visit my family*	√
Visit David's family	√
Go to work	√
Walk the dogs	√
Go to weddings	√
Go to funerals	√
Go to Christenings	√
Go to Morrisons/ASDA/Tesco	√
Get a promotion	√
Get more (useless) qualifications	√
Go down the pub	√
Do the washing/ironing/cleaning.	√
Go to work	√

How weary, stale, flat, and unprofitable seem to me all the uses of this world! Where was the man/boy who broke into the bakery and had sex amongst the flour bags? Who blagged his way into Napoleon's Nightclub? Who ended up shagging a Kate Bushalike in Turnpike Lane? Who leapt into a yellow sports car with two strangers and drove off into the London night? Where has he gone? What has been traded up? Why did what sounded like everything I'd ever wanted feel like it wasn't, actually?

Look, don't think I'm ungrateful. Don't get me wrong – in terms of security, stability, solvency, sociability all was good, so why was I feeling so….trapped? Stop fucking moaning! What else could you want? You're lucky! Mr. Lucky! Yet…and yet….

Anyway, I put my head down, did what I was told and got on with it. Months passed, turned into years…..

When John left, I went to tell my parents, of course. My Dad seemed nonplussed – like he couldn't understand what I was talking about, like he didn't really believe it WAS a relationship so *ergo* it couldn't be real and so what was I moaning about….

"OH. I quite liked him. Nice chap." And that was that.

A few weeks later, with Gill apparently keeping me safe from Hell and damnation, after I'd met David, I again when to see them and said: *"I've got a new…er..partner. He's really nice. Shall I bring him over next time?"*

"No. You won't."

"Why? He's a really nice chap!" (Did I REALLY say 'chap'?)

"I don't care. I said no."

"But you liked John, didn't you?"

I've met one of them. I won't do it again. That's the end of it."

And it was. That's how he was, the old bastard. Implacable. Intransigent. It was EIGHT YEARS before David and he met. It was the weirdest thing. We were in Truro and I rang my Mum from a call box (remember them?) and asked if she'd like to meet for a coffee. Poor old Mum – back to the clandestine meets, always having to come alone, although I DO think she rather enjoyed getting out for a few hours. I heard her say, *"I'm just going into to town to meet Nigel"*, and then there was a silence. Then she said it.

I emerged from the phone box, ashen faced. Kind of stumbling.

"What's the matter? Has someone died? What's happened?"

"Dad says he wants to meet you. We're to go to the house. Now."

So we went, me crapping myself – it felt like a Church Windows moment, and I couldn't get rid of those demons, now, some 30 years on and I felt like a child.

We arrived. Mum let us in, pale and anxious.

"He's through there," she said motioning us in. And so he was. Standing, hand extended, smiling.

"So, you must be David. Pleased to meet you." WHAT THE FUCK….??? Eight fucking years later, God speaks, we go running and he acts like nothing's happened, or peculiar or wrong about this situation. David, on the outside at least, seemed completely unfazed, smiling back, shaking hands whilst we, Mum and me, watched in astonished fascination.

After what seemed like three years, but was probably only about an hour, we left, with Dad saying, *"Any time you're passing, pop in! Bye for now. Bye!"* and me saying, *"What the fuck was that…..? "* and David saying, *"I don't know why you say those things about him. He's a nice old boy..".* We drove home in silence, apart from the *'Best Rock Ballads. Ever'* drowning out the confusion in my head.

My life as a housewife / breadwinner continued apace, ticking all the boxes above, even, now, the one with the asterisk. No more was I driven to family Weddings (we'd drunk champagne while 96 Liverpool fans were crushed to death), to be dropped off at the door and collected, drunk, later on, usually when it was dark. No more being dropped off for Sunday Lunches and collected, full of spuds and sorrow, bloated and sad, a few hours later. No. God had spoken and now all was well in the world. Well, only if I never spoke about my life, where I'd been, what I'd done. School was OK – Pillar of Society an' all - ; family was OK, David's family was OK. But nothing to do with love, relationships, 'being together'...it was all bollocks really and I don't know why I played the game other than, I suppose, to be able to operate 'normally' for Mum, although she was constantly on edge in case one of us said anything 'homosexual'. There was always a large pink elephant in the room. I think she was always quite relieved when we left, that nothing had kicked off and she'd only be left behind with the snarling man who would blame her for everything; the better and familiar option.

The weeks, the terms, the holidays, the months, the years; *'life slips by like a field mouse, not shaking the grass'*, as Ezra Pound so accurately said. Was I happy? Yes. And no. Was I sad? Yes. And no. I just... WAS. Clouds with occasional sun. Or the other way round. My edges were becoming flatter, my spontaneity was disappearing. The waters were flat and calm.

The one thing that saved me, made me feel alive though, in spite of the routine nature of the job and its increasingly excessive demands as the years went by, was TEECHIN. I loved being with the kids. Their spirit was young and uncomplicated and life was new and bright and I could be a part of that; *WAS* a part of that.

When I started back in school full time, after leaving London, it was still 1988. Baker hadn't been Ed. Sec. long and hadn't fucked up my universe yet. I continued to 'do the show right there!!' I'd find a coin on the road, take it in and say, *"Look what I found! Whose pocket did it fall from? Where has it been….?"*

And I'd do an English lesson on that – original, non-proscribed, free from judgement and tick boxes. Maths? Oh, times tables practice is it? *"Don't groan – let's go outside and march round the playground – ok – four groups of eights please! Ten groups of four.."* It was fun, it was anticipated, it was effective, it was memorable. I will NOT get into a discussion over the National Curriculum; other than to say it was a monumental fuck up. It fucked the lessons, the spontaneity, the fun and the creativity. It fucked my children's confidence – the painters who would never 'be a 3 in Science'; my poets who would never 'be a 4 in Maths'. And, it fucked a whole generation of brilliant, gifted and dedicated teachers who lost heart and faith in what they were doing and, refusing to become a tick machine, left the profession. A whole generation. Replaced by inexperienced and cheap labour. To all of you, my friends and colleagues, who were beaten, driven out by the new Men, the corporate ethos, the new heads whose vision you no longer fitted - I weep for you for having your life's work belittled, devalued and made irrelevant in this Brave New World. Enough! I will not mention the TEN folders every teacher in the land was given, in which all our lesson plans were set out, minute by minute, one for each subject, at a cost of SIXTY THREE MILLION POUNDS that, a year or two later were scrapped! And we were given new ones. Over and over as each new Education Minister sought to make their mark: Kenneth Baker, John MacGregor, Kenneth Clarke, John Patten, Gillian Shephard, David Blunkett, Estelle Morris...Buffoons all of them, pandering to politics and toadying to their Masters in Westminster, pretending to know what they were doing, while the morale and performance of the nation's children plummeted. It didn't work then, and is not working still, in 2015 with a minister, after Michael Gove ('SIR', for his services to Education!!!!), Nicola Morgan who has NO educational background at all! No matter! She'll just do as she's told....

There. See? See what happens? I told you not to get me started! Although, actually it IS relevant to this story. To backtrack....

As all this developed, as it all went from Teaching to EDUCATION, and I climbed the Career Ladder – ending up as Deputy Head before I left, as well as being on numerous Committees and Boards, the only thing that really gave me real joy, any sense of still being able to do what I loved was the Drama productions I did. Every year, Year 6, the oldest class of 10 and 11 year olds and I would mount a full scale musical. I did 12 in all, one each year I was there. So, this is for you

Jonno, who couldn't spell, but could break dance like a boss; this is for you Mary, who couldn't read very well but could sing like Charlotte Church or Beyoncé – you chose which; this is for you Paul, who only got a Level 1 for handwriting because he was left handed and all his work was illegible and therefore unconsidered but who could play 'Wonderwall' on his guitar in front of a hall full of adults; this one's for you Peter, who hated and detested Maths, felt stupid and a failure in the Maths tests which I was obliged to deliver at 09.20 on Monday mornings, apologetically, because it just didn't work for you and I am truly sorry for making you feel like that, Yes, for *you* Peter, who could rap like 50Cent and knew all the words to *'At the End of the Day'* from 'Les Mis' and for all the others I had the privilege to work with who will never be scientists or statisticians but who loved Drama Club and singing and dancing and saying: "LOOK! I CAN DO THIS!" and seeing Mum and Dad weep with joy to see them happy, for a while, at school. Here's to all 350 of you who went through that process with me; the singers and groaners, the tappers and clodhoppers but the ones who didn't care and found a home where no one judged them, no one gave them marks out of 10, made them do it again because it wasn't spelled right or was too untidy, or stay in a playtime to finish the work that had been too hard to finish in too short a time but that was just tough shit because I have another box to tick after playtime – here's to you all and I should be thanking YOU for keeping me sane in a world that was changing out of all recognition and out of control.

'Not allowed to comfort a crying child'? 'Not allowed to pick up a child who had fallen over'? 'Not allowed to sit and have a boyfriend chat with a confused Y6 girl'? 'Not allowed to mop up the blood from a grazed knee'? For me, this new world was madness – they were children, we were *in loco parentis*. Absolute bollocks. I ignored it anyway – how can you stand by while a 5 year old howls on the ground, pouring blood, while you wait for the designated First Aid person to come, who had run out of latex gloves because the budget didn't allow any more, so she wasn't allowed to help anyway? I didn't. At the very least I'd get on the floor and comfort them, hug them. Health and Safety be fucked. Fuck right off and when you get there, fuck off some more.

The world I knew as an enabler, a teacher, a story teller, a weaver of magic, a kindly man who gave my heart and skills to making these kids fit for the world was vanishing, disappearing under new legislation, appearing almost weekly:

new rules, new curricula, lists of tick boxes, score sheets, assessment files – where was the time to teach? Not to mention marking, planning (which became a labyrinthine exercise in time keeping) and classroom preparation. Oh yes, and trying to have a life. Even Drama club was failing to feed me – it was harder and harder to find four hours a week for rehearsal, upon which I insisted to maintain the quality of the productions. By this time, and God knows why, I was training to get my NPQH (two years of hard slog, for fuck all. Never used, even when I was still in teaching, never helped me get a job, a monumental waste of resources, though I DO have a rather splendid certificate, signed by Estelle Morris, who was Education Minister that week); I was Deputy Head, Staff Development Officer, ICT Co-ordinator, History Co-Ordinator, Key Stage 2 Team Leader, Manager of G.E.S.T. Budget, (you can look this stuff up, if you can be arsed) Appraisal Team leader, Teacher Governor, Chairman of School Council, Chairman of Curriculum Sub – Committee, Child Protection Officer….oh yes, and doing half the Head's work because he was either out at meetings, building his Empire or decided it was "good for my career development" AND teaching a Y5 class of THIRTY FIVE 9 / 10 year olds (Lying fucking bastard 'No classes bigger than 30' Labour party), TWELVE of who had special needs statements, but only ONE teaching assistant. Julie, I bless you for holding back the tide….

Trying to put on massive productions after school, look after my partner, go to rehearsals for Phoenix Drama, which by now was mounting THREE productions a year, was all rather taking its toll. I firmly believe that if I hadnt seen the teeny two line ad. in the Times Ed that day, I would have had some sort of breakdown. I was in crisis.

Meanwhile, back in la-la land…..

When I was 36, it was a very good year….it was a very good year, for luvvies to ply their trade upon the boards (if you sing along, it really does fit…!)….I joined the local Drama group (a decision that was to cause SOOOO much trouble later) and suddenly, instead of just 'helping out backstage', suddenly found myself with the lead role in *'AN INSPECTOR CALLS'*, a play WAY beyond the skillset of the group and one that should never have even been considered. Apart from having TWO WEEKS rehearsal and learning a 55 page script (which should've been a warning – how could that have been good enough?) I was 36, 'Arthur Birling' was late middle aged. Hmmm, what can we do? I know! Put some white talc in my hair and draw some wrinkles on in black eyebrow pencil. Oh, and put a cushion up me tux. Yes, dear reader, it was dire. Just the worst am- dram stuff….the stuff I swore I would never get involved in. What it *DID* do though, was get me an *in*…..the next thing I know I had been asked to choose the next play, AND direct it. That was more like it.

'Abigail's Party' fitted the bill nicely –one of the things I did was to choose a play which we could actually cast with people of the right(ish) ages and the varying amount of skill and stagecraft. Here began my deep and abiding, often troubling, mostly rewarding, friendship with Ann, who was bloody marvellous as the horrendous 'Beverly Stern'. Apart from much hilarity (known only to us, and me tearing out what remaining hair I had as 'Tony' got lost in the dungeon of Bodmin Jail, in which we were performing, with Ann whispering as *sotto voce* as she could whilst not trying to set off the echoes that would boom through the subterranean tunnels, "TONYYYYY! I mean PEEEETER….you're ON! NOW Now Now Now Now Now!!!", then returning to stage, adlibbing like a trooper, saying, *"Hmmm, Tony's a long time, Ange. I'll just go and see where he is…"* and going offstage again while the rest of the cast desperately ate stale nibbles and asked how Abigail *really* was….), it was a great show, well received – in spite of its apparent froth, it's quite a challenging work. It was reviewed well and enabled me to do pretty much what I wanted (or, believed to be right). Next, we did a play, *'Bitter Sanctuary'*, set in a refugee camp next. We'd constructed the ceiling of the 'barracks' out of a sheet of black fertilizer sack plastic. Unfortunately, I hadn't factored in the heat of the spots above it and as the play progressed, the ceiling got lower and lower, as the plastic sagged. I just pretended it was deliberate and meant as a metaphor for the world closing in around the refugees, their lives narrowing…..

More plaudits for the acting and directing, with the local press taking notice. We then decided to do Genet's *'The Maids'*, a 3-hander with my best 2 women. The Committee hated the idea, said Bodmin 'wasn't ready for it', and so we said: *"Fine, we're leaving and going out on our own"*.

Phoenix Drama was born from the ashes of the old company; all the cast came with me and we went on to fine things, taking on challenge after challenge:

I had a trumpet back then and I'm blowing it here, for myself and for the people with whom I shared the tears and joys of working on these wonderful plays. Wherever you all are, I thank you for sharing your spirit, dedication and humour with me on this dramatic journey.

Plays Wot I Have Done.

I was using Phoenix, as I suspect were most of us, as an escape. Two nights a week rehearsal, then three nearer play week, then a whole week. A week or two off then back to readings for the next. We kept up this crazy pace for years, not daring to look behind us, not wanting to be ordinary. Off to Summer Schools where we could be who we wanted. Nobody's wife / husband / mother / boyfriend / colleague. We were just actors, singers and dancers – and the lucky ones were all three. Wedding rings were 'stashed, names changed, middle names used, nicknames made up…no history, fresh minted where we could indulge our passion, sing, dance, smoke drink, swear, cry, moan….just be free for one glorious, shining week. They were the best of times, the worst of times. Hot- housed, emotions ran much higher without the brake of our normal lives. People shagged, had flings. I did too – nothing serious, just a quickie, cocks that passed in the night, when I was pissed. When he was pissed. When nobody cared and nobody judged. A cocoon which, like summer, was over all too soon and we'd return home to the places we'd come from, promising to write forever and stay in touch (and never did, until the following year when we all met up again) though some real and lasting bonds were made. I have a dear dear friend whom I met through Summer School and if you're reading this – I thank you for your abiding love. Boop boop be doop.

All the while, my relationship with Ann deepened. We were the best in the group. That's not boastfulness, that's just a fact. We also were the most committed and hardest working, which is why we always got the lead roles – because they were the hardest, the longest, required the most learning and commitment. There is a play called *'To'*, where the two actors play all fourteen parts – extremely demanding, extremely complex for the actors and Ann and I did it and did it well. We took it on a mini tour and also performed it on the professional stage at The Drum in Plymouth. When I hear

My love,
There's only you in my life
The only thing that's right

My first love,
You're every breath that I take
You're every step I make….

anywhere now, any time, I still remember the dry mouthed terror we felt, as the opening music, *'Endless Love'*, played, waiting backstage to go on and start….but we did it and it was wonderful. Ann and I hurtled closer. *'When She Danced'*, a play about Isadora Duncan required me to learn the entire part in Russian, as Sergei Esenin, her lover. It was terrifying – normally if you dry, you can ad lib, say something approximate, or be prompted by your fellow actor, but this – no one knew it but me, no one was able to get me out the shit if I got lost. And, I am pleased to say, I didn't! Not once! It's a very clever play – read it, if you get a chance. 'Sergei' and 'Isadora' had a fair bit of fondling and snoggin…..our relationship deepened. The last play we did together, before I had to leave, was the massive Arthur Millers *'Broken Glass'* – hugely demanding parts for us both. I had a terrible and inexplicable problem getting my lines down – there were so many of them, in Bronx patois – and so Ann came to help, where that was usually David's 'job'. We spent days and nights together at

Summer Schools, rehearsing constantly….and you know what? We fell in love. She was married, I'm a homosexual so it was never going to work, was it? Nevertheless, we had a fierce passion, a burning need to be in each other's presence, justifying it in the name of Drama. And, yes David loathed her. Did the same stuff he did with Gill, tried to freeze her out, but she was made of stronger stuff. It was a stormy sea we sailed; she had her own troubles and demons and the type of plays we took on served only as catalysts, excoriating and flaying us just a little each time, peeling back skin and revealing truths that were hard to bear. We were in the wrong lives. Deep down we knew, but we were both creatures of habit, developed over years, unwilling to face that truth. Obviously we couldn't be together, didn't WANT to be together, but our 'other life' showed us the possibilities, the place we could exist in joy. So we continued in this *faux* life, and gradually both our partners began to lose their grip….eventually, Ann left her husband and her old life and went travelling, found her peace in other lands and eventually alighted in Canada, and is being the person she truly is. I like to think that the time we spent in Phoenix, where Art mirrored Life, and the times we spent acting out alternatives, were a part of the change she became. It was a far from easy time; the only time I was free of the whirlpool of feelings – feelings of passion for Ann, confusion for David, disappointment for teaching – was during rehearsals and play nights. When I was someone else. And THAT, dear reader, is the key. THAT is why, I think that being a Luvvie, if I trace it back over the years, through the school plays, all the stuff at Balls Park (HAHAHAHHAAA BALLS PARK), the Drama Club, and the intense workout of being in a Phoenix production, was so important for me. BECAUSE, FOR A SHORT TIME, I WAS SOMEONE ELSE. BOOM! RIGHT THERE. So what the fuck am I supposed to do with that? And I knew INSTANTLY what and why – it was *him*, his loathing of his son, for being in the SSU, for being mis-created, for being an embarrassment. Not for being a decent man, a good teacher, an accomplished actor, a holder of a Cert. Ed (credit), a recipient of the NPQH...none of those good, wholesome, societally good things that I had to offer. I was a disgusting queer, and nothing more. So, being '*Sergei*', '*Phillip Gelburg*', '*Bob Jackson*', '*The Landlord*' et al - *was* that just me, NOT being that person that my father found so repulsive? Was that all it was? I hope not – it brought such joy, such fulfilment – I want to remember it as something positive, not as a way just NOT to be me. But, the more I examine this idea, the clearer it becomes. I owed him nothing. He did to me what may be regarded as one of the most awful things a parent might do: he rejected me because of what he considered, and did so to his dying day, to be wrong, immoral, (*YOU* talk to *ME* about morals, you child beater), against nature and that, because I CHOSE it, I should suffer the consequences of that rejection (NOT, I should remind you, by my Mother), and disgust. That's pretty hard to handle when a) I didn't choose it (Why would I? Why would any gay person make a choice that inevitably leads to sorrow to some degree, vilification, abuse and often harm?) and b) it was terribly difficult thing and I really really needed his support, his hand upon my shoulder guiding me through the maelstrom of finding my sexuality, telling me it would be OK, and that he'd love me, whatever. This, as you know, was not what happened…

So, I have decided to OWN my luvviness as a badge of honour, *sa 'Hullo Clouds, Hullo Sky' and skip about like a gurl*… It was NOT an escape (well, it was, but from other things); I did not want to be someone else. And he could go fuck himself. It was such a balancing act; he would never and did never, in all the 19 years I lived there, come to 'the queer's house'. He'd drop my Mum off, who came often, and then pick her up at a prearranged time, from the end of the road, and yet – he'd invite us round to HIS house, for tea and biscuits; he and David would get on like bosom buddies or, even more painful to me, like a long lost son. We never mentioned the **Q** Word, EVER. So, conversation was reduced to the weather and what had been on telly (censored before we discussed it. No allusion to *you know what* in any programmes mentioned. *'Dallas'* was deffo off the list…), with Mum hovering anxiously in the background, making tea that nobody really wanted. So, as I said, he could go fuck himself.

To repeat the mantra I had created so long long ago, to protect myself,

I AM GAY.

I AM A GAY MAN.

I AM A GOOD PERSON.

I HAVE WORTH.

I HAVE LOVE AND GIVE IT FREELY.

I AM A GAY MAN.

And therefore, if he (or anybody else) didn't like it, well...their loss. I'm a nice bloke; a little effeminate, sometimes acerbic, open hearted and I'm kind to animals and small children. The same as you, you who are reading this. Where I put my willy is none of your business, nor relevant to having a decent relationship with you, if ever we should meet.

Where was I? Oh yes. Stuck. Lost. Bored. Nice house, good job, faithful (I assumed) lover. Stop bleddy moaning. Actually I wasn't moaning. I just *was*. Day after day, week after month after year. Boom! Up the ladder of success, although that was weighing more and more heavily. I had a better income, but less and less time to enjoy it. David kept the books. We never seemed to have enough money, which was a strange thing (although when I questioned this, I was told I *'could do the fucking accounts myself if I wanted'*, eliciting the reply. *"Ooooh, I wouldn't know what to do. No, you do them"* Right answer.) but we also never had enough time to go anywhere. We went on holiday once. Once. In all that time. Spain it was. Very nice too. I had become 'Mr. Normal'. Wasn't that what I'd always craved? I'd done my thing, spread my seed, boogied my nights away, shagged myself sore – now I had a nice, normal life. Most people would be grateful And I was. But with each play, each Summer School, I went further away from suburbia and towards something....unattainable. And I didn't even know what it was.

CHAPTER FOUR.

LOST FOR WORDS.

In which our hero's heart breaks once more and he finds solace with the Angels.

'Unchained Melody.'

by Annie Lennox No1. June 14th 1996

My love, my darling, how I hungered for your touch, when it was too late.

~ ~ ~

We went shopping a lot, to buy things we neither wanted nor needed. I became known as 'Imelda Bray' after my collection of shoes that over-ran the porch. Coats. Jumpers, all folded, in colour order. Ornaments. Stuff. Stuff. By now, both Sam and Lisa were gone so we had more free time! Yay! Shopping without having to get back to the car. Poor Sam had eighteen months with us; a happy time he would not have had and he was loved and adored by all who met him. But cancer got him; it got to the point he could no longer swallow the mush I was feeding him with by hand and so we made that endless silent journey to the vet, where he died in my arms. I scattered ashes up on the hill (when it wasn't too windy – he never liked the wind – it makes his ears flap in an alarming manner). Poor Mr. Fizzle, with his big feet and his big heart.. Gone too soon.

So, to fill the dog shaped holes, we bought things. Stuff. Stuff we didn't need. On June 14th, in 1996, we went to Truro, to get some stuff, probably. We had a meal quite early on, went to the pub, had a couple of pints and headed back home.

Passing Threemilestone, David said,

"Do you want to stop and pop in on Mum and Dad?" Not *'your'* mum and dad. Another bit of me he owned. How strange he'd adopted (and been adopted by) my Father, who loathed *me*.....

"No, I don't think so." I couldn't stand the *faux* polite bollocks, the making up interesting things to talk about – David shagging me in the cave on Perranporth Beach was off limits, I suppose, so no, I didn't want to. *"I'd rather just get home."*

"OK, suit yourself."

So we drove on, along the by-pass, past the end of their road, past their house, inside which as we passed, my Mother lay dead on her bed.

"Put the radio on? We've run out of CDs and I don't want to open any of the ones we bought today." Stuff. Stuff.

'Common People' playing. *"I bleddy hate Pulp. Try another station."*

'A Whiter Shade of Pale.'

"Oooh, I like Annie Lennox. D'you remember the Eurythmics were around when we met?"

"Hmm."

"We tripped the light fandango, turned cartwheels cross the floor..." I wailed. Blimey, those beers were a bit strong. *'I was feelin' kinda seasick, but the crowd called out for more... doo doo doo doo dadada......"*

And my Mother lay dead.

"I'm putting pirate.fm on now. Oh YESS! UNCAHINED MELODY!! I LOVE THIS! IT'S NUMBER ONE! I'M NOT SURPRISED MIND. DID WELL THEM SOLDIERS EH?"

"Can you stop yelling?"

"Sorry. Just love this song. 'Time goes by, so slowly and time can mean so much. Are you still MIIIIIIINE?'"

David drove in silence.

Lay dead.

When we got home, I raced upstairs to empty my Stella – filled bladder, and coming back out of the bathroom, notice the answer machine flashing. Thirteen messages? THIRTEEN? Alarm bells jangled faintly.

I picked up, pressed play: *'It's Rosemary Ring me."* *"It's Rosemary. Ring me'*, and variations of this. Thirteen times. I rang her.

"Hello? Rose? Sorry, we were…."

"I got some awful bad news. Your mother's dead." She was never very good with grammar, I thought. As you do.

"Eh?"

"Sorry, but your Mother's dead."

Now, I remember very little about the next few hours. I DO remember saying: *"What sort of dead?* And then saying to David *"she says your mother's dead. Do you think we'd better go round there? Poor Ruth…"*

David came up, took the phone from my hand, spoke briefly and then said, *"No, it's YOUR Mother. Rosemary wouldn't be ringing me about MY Mother, would she?"* Ever logical, even then. *"Get in the car."*

And we drove back to Truro, back to the house we'd passed not an hour ago. My memory of that journey was both blurred and crystal clear. My ears were muffled, the road noise was silent.

"STOP! STOP THE CAR." We pulled over. *"I can't her voice. I can't hear her voice. I can't hearhervoiceIcan'thearhervoiceIcan'thearhervoice…."* And then trailed away into silence. We drove. In slow motion towards some horror I as yet couldn't comprehend.

The house was cloaked in a kind of deadness. Everything was still. People were moving in slow-motion around Dad who was sitting in the corner, looking tiny, tiny, stunned, smashed. Debs was there, Barrie, Rosemary, and Sandra, all busying themselves doing nothing, in silence.

"She's gone, boy. She's gone." That was all he said, his voice reedy and worn. I didn't know what to do, physically. His leg were stretched out on to a pouffé and I just sat on them; they were so thin I could've snapped them in two. Still I said nothing. I didn't know who this was, this man being emotional with me. All I could do was reach over and lay my hand on his face. It was cold. He said no more.

Mum, according to Rose, who of course knew everything, had been ironing that afternoon and had felt a bit tired. She went to have a lie down and simply died. Dad, a couple of hours later, took her in a tray of tea and found her cold and dead on the bed. At that moment, according to her, later the next day in the pub, Debs had arrived and heard screaming, went into the bedroom to find Dad kneeling over Mums body, shaking it violently, slapping her in the face, shouting "WAKE UP WAKE UP!!. PAT WAKE UP!!" Her head was flopping violently up and down and her hair, her beautiful always – groomed hair was flying all about. As she approached, Mum's teeth flew out of her gaping mouth onto the bed and she ran. I don't know how the news broke. Maybe Debs rang Rose? Her mother? Maybe Dad did later, I don't know, but in the time between David and I driving past and back, she'd been carried away in a body bag, and I never saw her.

'She'd gone', in all senses of the word – from the house, from our lives and from the world. It's so hard now, almost 20 years on to fully describe how these first hours and days were. I guess, anyone reading this will attest to a similar experience – it was just sort of floating, floating through the days. That evening, we, Gill, Debs and me, found some gin in the cupboard that they'd bought for Queen Victoria's coronation of something and we drank it, right from the bottle, passing it round, like proper seasoned vagrants, necking it straight from the bottle until what was real and what was pissedness all became one surreal, misty family gathering. But still no noise. No drunken whispering, no enquiries about how people were. It was just silent, just that 'gollop' that liquid makes in a bottle as it is gulped from and passed on. We were drunk, and we were numb. Best result all round. Apparently Barrie then decided it was Gill's 'turn' to look after Dad and we all left. I have no recollection of leaving, only being full of gin and lead, too heavy to move.

The following week was just full of fuzz. I drank a huge amount, as if when I sobered up she'd be there, moaning at me for being in such a state and it had all been a terrible mistake. But it wasn't. "She's gone, son" was the only true thing.

MYOCARDIAL INFARCTION. How grand! How fuck off 'n *die*! Which of course she had. Fucked off and died. According to the autopsy she had an undiagnosed heart problem. There'd been something wrong with her heart and no one knew. Not even her. Now there was something wrong with all of ours – they were all broken. Who was going to fix US, eh? *EH?*

Gill had done her 'shift' and I said I'd do mine. Clearly I was in zombie mode as I would never have volunteered to go there, back to that house, to the place, the world as I perceived it, the world that my little, sharp tongued, perspicacious mother once inhabited. Dad was no use, no conversation was to be had. Gill and he were talking in the front room and I went to the bedroom. To her dresser, her red, too – big – for- her – face glasses still lying there, one arm open, never to be peered through again, while watching *'Corrie'* or *'The News at Ten'* or laughing inside, but silently, as tears ran down her face at *'Morcambe and Wise'*, before being laid on the mantelpiece while she went to make their cocoa. Her powder compact, her brush, a few stray grey hairs bouncing in the bristles, as my breath disturbed them as I pressed it to my face to breath in her scent. Her talc, Max Factor, pink and inert, and now forever to be left unscraped. I kept that compact for years; if I cracked open the lid, she would flood out, borne on a wave of sorrow and regret…..

….regret that I didn't know what her religious beliefs were; what her favourite colour was; what she did during the war; how many boyfriends she'd had; what she thought of Granny Bray; what her Mum was like before she became 'my Nan'; what school she went to; where she'd been on holiday before I was born; why she married my Dad; what she was like at school – was she clever? Was she naughty? What were her favourite subjects? Regret I'd never asked her these things because I was going to ask her dreckly and now it was too fucking late and now I would never know stuff. Fuckfuckfuckfukfuck. OWWWWWW I hurt.

She was 19. Now gone. How?

The room was so silent. The bed where she lay dying, alone and nobody knew, where nobody came and said goodbye or smiled as she left us, was smoothed out, the storm of sheets created by my incoherent father as he shook her and slapped and knocked the teeth out of her cold mouth had been smoothed out, all evidence of the terrible moments erased. Just the faint smell of 'Tweed' and powder.

She came to me that night. As sure as I am sitting here writing this, I know this to be the truth. Dad had gone to bed, it was 11.11 on the clock, the room suddenly chilled to zero (just like in the movies) and there she was. Well, not in a whooo whoooo sort of way, but just a clear and definite presence. And she said; *"I will never let you fall"*. And you never have. It was joyful and wonderful and peaceful and terrifying and then it was done. The air got warm and an hour had passed.

Because she had been taken away, I wanted to see her. Once more. And again. And again, but time was limited and they were going to take her away, away to a place I would never be able to see her or touch her again. Her body was now in the morgue in the hospital in Truro. Sorry – 'chapel of rest'. I wanted to go. I WOULD go, and nothing my Dad could say would stop me. It was up to me whether I would be upset – I was thirty fucking six years old. I could do what I liked. In the event, Dad Gill and I all went. We sat outside the door – the terrifying door behind which lay my Mother; far more terrifying than those glass doors of the Salisbury which had terrified me so many years ago. Plain, pale brown, giving no clue as to what sorrow lay behind.

"You can go in now," said a kindly voice, a voice made of brown, practiced in making little noise but whose words held all the anxiety in the world.

"Thank you," I said and stood. I turned to the other two. *"I want to go in on my own"*.

"You can't. You'll be too upset".

I almost told him to go and fuck himself, for the thousandth time, in my head, but Gill said: *"Let him go. He'll be OK"*.

I thank her for that little act of kindness at that dark and terrible time.

The door swung open, without a sound. Why is everything so silent? Then the second door stood in front of me, blank, unassuming, not telling of the despair and the lakes of tears that would have been shed in the room behind it.

I opened the door (shwwwsshhhhhhh, hinges moving silently, the door not touching the carpet) and walked through. I was like a puppet man, a little unarticulated spikey thing whose joints didn't work. The impulse NOT to enter was immense, but the knowledge that it was the last, the very last time I would see her, pushed me through and it swung silently shut behind me.

There she lay. A purple velvet cloth up to her collar bones, her hair beautiful, thin (she hated that) and set beautifully upon the pillow. I stood transfixed and realised that this was the first time, or at last the first time in many years that she wasn't looking beaten, afraid, troubled or tired. Yes, she looked at peace – everyone says that, but I mean it was *deeper*; it was that for the first time in god knows how long, people weren't causing her grief. Me included. I approached (why was I on tiptoe?) and came up to her body. Pale, smooth, still…wait! What was that? Peeping over the edge of the cover were black threads. I reached over and pulled it back a little, then more and then down to where her breastbone was. Stitches. Great black ugly stitches, holding together a great white gash where they'd cut her open. Cut her OPEN. CUT MY MOTHER FUCKING OPEN!! It was terrifying, shocking, yet somehow it wasn't OF her. It belonged to someone else's body. They would have seen her lummies. She would have been horrified. I replaced the cover quickly – being caught looking at my Mum's boobs was a most embarrassing thought.

After my breathing had slowed, I looked again. There she was. The woman who had suckled me, raised me, fought for me, cried over me, golden ear whizzed me, loved me, defended me, fed me, never gave up on me in the face of the fiercest opposition – dead. Breathless. Hearbeatless. Cold. I took her hand, held it. Cold, from the fridge where they'd kept her, with a label on her toe and a cleft through her body, stitched, neatly overstitched with black shiny thread. How I hated her then, in a flash of red, for leaving me, business unfinished, too much unasked and unsaid. For leaving me with HIM, without an ally, without someone to defend me, to silently say 'it's OK'.

'You haven't finished your job! YOU were supposed to go second! You created me, he thinks I'm an aberration and you just fucking LEAVE ME!!' All that in an instant, in a flash of self-pity, cos my Mummy wasn't there to protect me from the big bad world. And then gone.

"Sorry, Mum." I said. *"Sorry for being gay. Well, not for being gay, but for it causing you so much grief. We should've spoken more about it, should've discussed it more. Uncle Billy loved you, you know and so did Rod. Everyone you met did. Now you've buggered off. What are you like? Ah well. I probably would've too. But thanks for making the effort you did. SO, I'm off into the world, alone now. Well, Gill will look after me, I expect, so that's good…."*

I was crying now, the first real tears, silently (of course) drips on the end of my nose, in the creases of my mouth and a tear fell on her cheek and as I kissed it away, I realised that Gill was in the room, her concern aided by the silent door.

"Feel her Gill. Take her hand. It's a bit cold, but it's ok", and there we stood, orphans, one each side, lost and in a world with no touchstone or idea of how to proceed with our lives. And there we stood, brother and sister, stunned, helpless, each holding a pale cold hand of our dead mother. Oh! How I wanted it to slap me round the ear. Hold my cheek. But it just flopped back to bed when we lay them back, and arms around each other's neck, we stumbled from the horror that was the death of our mother.

No words were spoken or necessary on the way home. To the pastyless, Corrie – less house that echoed with her voice and smelled of her hair.

She was taken to the Funeral Directors next and once more we all filed in, all of us just grabbing one more chance….Dad, then Barrie, then Gill. I followed her in, unknown to her and sat quietly in the corner while she cradled her mother's head and sobbed into her hair. Eventually, sensing some kind of meltdown, I stood and led her gently away. Enough, enough now. It was leading nowhere except into hopeless despair and we needed to be in some kind of shape for the last stage of this ghastly process.

Wednesday, 21st June. 11.00. In loving memory of Patricia Helena Bray, it said on the front. A 'programme' for her funeral. A paper memorial to something I cannot clearly remember. I was asked to be one of the bearers and I just nodded dumbly. It couldn't get any more awful, so I agreed. We all turned up at the church (what irony!) and the hearse opened, and there she was – in her oaken box. What a waste of fucking money! She'd be fucking FURIOUS. The undertakers slid it out and we hoisted it on our shoulders. Man, heavy! Must be the wood, she was only titchy. Smells of wood. Nice. Sandra holding on to the doorframe, like Garfield, having to be prised off and dragged in side; my dear friends, Liz and Ann laying a comforting hand on my shoulder as we passed (an unforgettably kind gesture that meant more than they will ever know), passing down the aisle, resting the coffin on its bier, backing away rubbing my shoulder, sitting with the family (front row seats), singing the WORST hymns ever, trying to comfort dad (Me! More irony!), David sitting behind me with his hand on my shoulder, (Even more irony!), Gill sobbing, me seeing *her* sitting in the corner, looking really grumpy in her lime green suit, Dad throwing himself across the coffin and howling, howling howling….all these fractured memories…

…then, in the hearse, filled with fag smoke, a long long journey to the crem. for the final act. Another service, shorter – there were more people waiting; in, orate, burn, out, next – the click of the mechanism as the curtains began to slide along the rail, the clunk of the gears as the ratchets engaged to drag the £500 coffin with my dead mother inside into the flames. Stand, turn, exit into the sun. Go down the pub. See ya.

Actually we went back to the house, where Rosemary had laid on a 'do'; there was more quiche in that room than there was in whole of France. Cucumber sarnies, *vol au vents*, puff pastry sausage rolls sadly sat on plates, untouched – completely misjudged, though meant well. It was *party* food, fer Chrissakes and we really didn't feel much like partying. Dad had returned, silent and closed, to his chair in the corner and soon people stopped saying '*Sorry for your loss*' and '*She was a wonderful woman*' as it became increasingly clear he wasn't listening or caring. Gradually, the gate crashers (Granny Bray and Lylie would've loved it) and acquaintances left, leaving family – cousins and nephews, aunts and nieces, to sadly pinball around the room, pretending to want to talk, but really wondering when it would be possible to fuck off without appearing too rude. Liz and Ann, bless them, stayed for a while, one each side, propping me up, until they too left. Thank you, thank you both for an immeasurable act of kindness that day. Out came the gin (thoughtfully replenished by the gin fairies) and we – Gill, Sam, Barrie, Rose, Debs, Dad, David and me – went out to the garden to proceed with the business of the day, which was, in my case, to get properly drunk. Gill and Sam went to sit in the car where they held each other and sobbed and sobbed while they listened to a cassette of Mum's favourite, *The Carpenters;* the rest of us rolled fags and drank. Eventually, as we all knew he would, Barrie stood and tapped on his glass – his normal method of beginning his 'speech', the one he always made at 'do's' and parties and weddings (when it was none of his business usually) and that went on and on until everyone had lost the will to live – and began: "We all know why we're here. To honour a great lady who…" What? It's my Mother's funeral you wanker, not a retirement or a 100th birthday. My MOTHER. Who is DEAD!! So I stood too, with the help of

Debs and said (though the following had been recounted since as I was too pissed to remember it):

*"Shut the fuck up. Barrie. Boy Borrie. We're here because my Mum's dead. Our Mum's dead. Fuckin dead, so **YOU**…shut the fuck up with your speeches. She dead and I'm fuckin furious about it and I want it go back the way it was and I don't like it and I'm upset and let's just all have a little drink instead. 'To Mum' and I fucking fucking miss her…"* and by now I was howling and had to be led away into the house. The rest of the day eludes me. I hope I slept and that my speech goes down in family lore.

The days as an orphan passed (dead to my Father, my Mother now ash) and apart from the mournful day we all met again to have her ashes dumped in a £200 hole at the crem, it was all over. Three ghastly weeks that would change me, and the family, forever. I felt more alone than I ever had; I was unkind to my friends, and when I went back to work, having had two weeks off, 'with grief' as my wonderful doctor phrased it on my sick note, I was dull and inert. Everything was an effort. The stories we all took so much joy in at the day's end were now a marker of time to go back home where nothing was. Drama club was an effort, devising ways of delivering an utterly dull prescribed curriculum was an effort. I was lost, truly lost and there was an abyss that I was afeard to look into, for at the bottom lay the answer I didn't want to seek. Ann had looked and gone; it was to be another seven years before I did.

CHAPTER FIVE.

MINT EGY PARTRA VETETT HAL. LIKE A FISH OUT OF WATER.

In which our hero finally grows a pair, goes to live on Mars and finally begins to understand where his future lies. (Clue: It wasn't here).

'Castles In The Sky'.

Ivan Van Dahl. No.4 August 2001.

I was lost; wot's it all about, eh? Dunno. Really. Castles in the air.

~ ~ ~

One of the more influential people I met during my time with David – many people bump in to your ship and send it on a course unexpected – was Anna. She was (still is, of course) a homeopath, a sacral craniologist and channel to spirit. All of which, until I met her, I thought was a load of old bollocks.

This is not the place to go into to the ins and outs of whether you think this is guff or truth; whether it works or if it doesn't. I thought the former, now I know that, for me, it is the latter.

I was a prime candidate at this time to be sucked into a vortex of anything that would give me some hope, some belief that things would be OK again. The family was fractured, Dad was sat in the centre of his web was spinning lies and spitting poison at each of us in his grief and anger at not 'having gone first'. This he continued to do until he died, playing each of us off against the other, lying about each of us to the others, not thinking that of course we all talked to each other and were aware of his games. The family was rudderless now – strange to look back and see just how much power, in her quiet way, my Mother had had – and I particularly was anxious to find something to fill the gaping hole left in my centre. New shoes didn't do it, nor restaurants, nor CDs or stuff of any kind. Though we continued to buy it at an alarming rate, it was an empty, soulless pastime. I could've probably become a Moonie or a Scientologist or anything where someone would have said 'There there, come on, we can make it better…' I didn't want to *'pull myself together',* thank you very much. I needed an answer as to why my Mother, without so much as a by your leave, went to bed that afternoon and died. And to how I was supposed to recover and get on.

Living in Cornwall provided plenty of 'alternatives' – it was and always has been an intensely spiritual place and, boy, did I need me spirit fixed…. I began, due to Anna's open mind and willingness to talk to me, The Unbeliever, about what SHE believed, to have a think maybe there is something out there for me. I went to see a psychic – whilst not dismissing it, it didn't really do it for me. I went to see someone who talked to angels. No, not there either. Tarot. Nope. Meditation – nice but just made me sleepy. I was just a fiddler, a man on the edges, not really believing anything could help.

Then, I found reiki. Or rather, it found me. The last possible thing I ever thought came to save me. And, the Universe moving in the mysterious ways that it does, planted the seeds for the rest of my life. There it was, in the Cornish Guardian, which I hardly ever read: 'Talk. Reiki. Wadebridge Library'. It couldn't have been more parochial. Why would I bother with that? It was a Tuesday, EastEnders was on…nah. I'll stay in. And yet…..

I went. Jim Wildman, an unassuming hairy bloke, surrounded by a group of lost souls, who maybe didn't care about Sanjay and his clothes stall that he was trying to run with Gita….and I sat at the back and in that moment my life changed. Forever. He talked about reiki, what it is, what it does, its provenance, but I wasn't really listening. I was trying to understand the feeling that I had in my centre; a kind of insistent throbbing and I knew right there and then that reiki had found me, that reiki would fill the space left by my mother, that reiki would heal me (because it does) and that it would become my life's work. I had met the angels, in secret, on that grey plastic chair in the municipal library that evening. Of *course* I was going to be at that meeting, of *course* I was going to meet Jim, who became my Master and trained me during the next few years. As the talk progressed, I became aware that he was addressing everything he said directly to ME, like he knew, like he recognised his next protégé, and a cord of golden light held us together.

After the meeting, the small crowd dispersed and he lightly tugged on the cord and I crossed to him.

"I knew you would come," he said.

"So did I. I think. It sounds...erm...very interesting. Could we meet again maybe?"

"I have a training class next Saturday and I would like you to attend."

"I will. Yes. I will."

I don't want to labour this...this revelatory moment. You can look up reiki online, there's tons of information, but I didn't need to find out any more, you know? I just KNEW. It was like I had ALWAYS known this man, and that Mum dying had made the space for reiki to come in. Anyway, I went to the class the following Saturday and it was just extraordinary. We did the initiation where Jim transferred the healing gift to our hands and we were asked to practise, focus on what we felt, and whatever we did, Jim's eyes never left me. When we got a chance to practise on one of the group on the couch, I didn't need to be shown the 'positions' – I already knew them, placing my hot hands in the correct places without any doubts, and it was wonderful, ecstatic. When the class ended, he said: *"Can you wait behind a moment?"*

When we were alone he said:

"I have been doing this for many years and I rarely have met someone so untrained that is so deeply connected with spirit. I would be honoured to take you on as a student. If you will have me."

And so, just like that, I became a reiki healer and over the next two years completed my training with Jim and became a Reiki Master. The funny thing is, I never saw him again. It was like he was invented to give me the opportunity to find my true self and carry on the work. I had been given a purpose, a new lease of life and my 'other life' was seeming less and less relevant. It felt now like I had stuff to do, though I didn't quite know what.

I'd really really had enough of school. It bore no resemblance to what I loved and knew. I was desperately tired, and rudderless. I'd left Phoenix, as I could no longer function – something had to give and being a Luvvie didn't pay the bills. Unless you're Ian McKellan or sumfink. I missed it, and Ann (or at least her bright spirit and the fun we had together, which included not being at home). Now, I was there all the time, living with my Dad. Being belittled, controlled, managed. None of which I realised or could articulate; if there was a household job to be done, I was forbidden to attempt it - *"You'll only mess it up. We'll get someone in"* – just like 40 years ago. Small and wee. Obedient. And bored.

Funny, innit? How you just don't know things? I didn't know just how I had got myself deep into this controlled environment – it seemed the norm. I didn't know what was being done to me and it wasn't till after, after 'What I Did', that anyone told me. It is so clear, looking back, that all my doomed relationships followed the same pattern: older men, surrogate Fathers but one who loved me and didn't loathe me for being a homosexualist; who controlled me, told me how to be and what to do, cos that's what Dads do, and that's why I did it…..oh you foolish child! It was NEVER going to work – you can't fuck your Dad! But it was what I was doing – being loved by these father figures. First prize in the 'Most Pathetic Needy Twat Contest'.

Is that all there is?

If that's all there is my friends

Then let's keep dancing

Let's break out the booze and have a ball

If that's all there is….

Yes, Peggy Lee. It seems so. But I couldn't even to do that, without disapproval. How did I get here?......

Spring Term, 2001. Same old, same old. Feeling like I was going to implode…. What's the use of this job if its killing me? I'm a reiki Master and it seemed to mean nothing, although Jim did say reiki *knows*…..maybe it wasn't my time. Maybe it had to 'cook', harden, and when the time as right, for me, it would burst forth in all its healing glory. Right now, it felt like a waste of time.

Lunchtime. Scotch egg and chips. Comfort food. Pick up the Time Ed Supp. Hundreds of ads, great blaring calls to go and teach, get a promotion, make a difference! I thought I did, once upon a time, now I was overburdened, overworked and listless. No good to me, no good to the kids.

'Have you ever thought of teaching in Eastern Europe', said the teeny weeny ad, sandwiched between dozens of other teeny weeny ads. *'Call this number'.* Just leapt out. Boom. Erm..no. not really. Bell rings, Science. Deep joy. Then PE then English then rehearsal. Plod plod plod.

Rehearsal went well, drove home, had tea, splat in front of the telly, dozed off, started awake, marked tomorrow's English books I'd forgotten twice, went to bed, got up, drove to school, made coffee….. *'Have you ever thought of teaching in Eastern Europe'*….

"Hello? Oh yes, I saw your ad in the Times Ed. Can you tell me a bit more, please?"

Bell rings, get kids in, registration, Maths for 20 minutes, pack up, handwriting practice. Etfuckingcetera.

At home that evening, I said, *"David. Have you thought about living abroad for a while? You know, if I got a job somewhere, say…. Hungary?"*

And to my utter astonishment, he said: *"That's an interesting thought. How?"*

So I recounted my conversation of that morning, not really believing a word that I was saying: teach English in a University in Hungary. HAHAHHAAAAA!

"The bloke is based in Barnstaple. He wants to interview me." I was expecting a bollocking for not having asked permission but no, I was told to ring back and arrange it. And that, dear reader, was the start, the first moments of my new life, and of the end of my relationship, though I didn't know that then.

To cut a long and rather bizarre story short, I went for an interview (two, actually) and I just knew, KNEW, that this would be the right thing to do, in spite of everyone at school going; *"What??? You're doing WHAAAAAAT??? Are you mad???"* but knowing I absolutely was not. Their main source of astonishment was based around money. My salary was to drop from around £1800 a month to £200. What was really strange was that this didn't bother me in the least. There was a free flat, with just phone calls to pay for. Work, apparently was just a short walk away, and everyone in the Language Dept spoke excellent English. Which was lucky, as Hungarian is known to be one of the most difficult languages to learn, in the world.

Here's part of a fairy story:

Egyszer egy félkegyelmű ember kiment az erdőbe fát vágni.

Ahogy fát vágott, egyszer csak ásított egy nagyot.

Nagyon megijedt, mert azt hallotta, hogy aki egymás után háromszor

ásít, az meghal.

Dolgozott tovább, de hamarosan másodszor is ásított, sőt harmadszor is.

No, ha háromszor ásított, akkor ő most halott, gondolta a félkegyelmű.

Lefeküdt hát az erdő közepén a földre és nem mozdult.

Otthon várta a felesége a vacsorával, de a félkegyelmű nem jött haza.

Az asszony meg a szomszédok keresni kezdték.

Kimentek az erdőbe, s meg is találták a félkegyelműt.

How on Earth is anyone supposed to pronounce any of it? What do all those funny marks do? I recognised nothing, NOTHING that would tell me how to say this, not any clue whatever as to the meaning of a single word. In French, Spanish, Italian – you can hazard a guess at least as to what it *might* be about, but…..

Just in case you're interested and want to use it in future, here's the bare bones of the story, translated by my Hungarian friend:

Once there was a nitwit (a kind equivalent of an idiot) who went to the forest to cut some wood. As he was cutting the woods he yawned a big one (I'm not quite sure how to translate this…)he got really frightened because he had heard that the person who yawned three times one after the other would die.

He went on working, but soon after that he yawned for the second time and even for the third time. Well, if he had already yawned three time, then he must be dead, thought the nitwit. He laid down in the middle of the forest and did not move.

His wife was waiting for him with his dinner but the nitwit did not go home. She together with their neighbours started to look for him. They went to the forest and finally they found him. To be continued…….

No. I thought not.

I don't feel it has much purpose to write and write about that year in detail, but it's important in the fact that of how it changed me. I went from a lost boy to a hero. I went from a person who had no worth to someone whose worth was recognised. I was valued and respected for what I did; people were grateful for the teaching they received. It felt all very strange! Just like the Olden Days...

It was a most unlikely scenario, mind. I had expected to remain in Bodmin, restricted and sad, suppressed and depressed, comfortably off but with no value. Well, for ever, I suppose. The new car, the point on the pay scale, all had come to mean less and less; it was getting to the point where there was no time to actually enjoy the fruits of my labours. So this quantum leap, this paradigm shift in my thoughts was a massive surprise – not least to me. Mostly people were supportive and wished me well, not voicing their opinions on the complete lunacy of it; people were already jostling for position for the space I was leaving; fer fuck's sake, the body wasn't even cold....

We packed up our stuff, rented the house out, found out where this 'ere 'Kecskemét' was on the map and set off, in the middle of one night, on a bus bound for London, barely able to carry the luggage we'd brought as we had no idea how long our stuff would take. We arrived at Ferihegy airport (rather alarmingly, it seemed to be just a field) in the middle of Summer, the day of the Budapest Grand Prix. August 19th, 2001. The day I went to Mars. The plane had been full of stupid English twats, all pissed up, and embarrassing themselves, pinching the stewardesses' arse, bound for the race. We landed in sweltering heat, wearing about six layers of clothes and winter coats, trying to bring as much as we could carry. Including my guitar, which was the very last thing off the plane and I was by now in a state of near panic as I had no clue where to go, what to do or how to ask. Eventually, it appeared, and as we were the only ones left, the man brought it me, said something utterly unintelligible and we set off, south to where we were to be living and I was to be teaching for the next year. I hadn't even completed my TEFL exams. *"Oh, never mind!"* they said....

As we travelled down through an utterly alien landscape, I began to realise what a MASSIVELY STUPID thing I had done, really without adequate preparation. I didn't even really know where Hungary WAS, let alone what it was like. I didn't know it was going to be like this....all weird and brown and dusty and miserable looking. As we got out of the city in to the countryside, with storks nesting on the lampposts (how cool!), the landscape changed – rural is a bit of an understatement; Houses in ruins, homesteads, dry barren gardens where chickens scratched and disconsolate children played in the dust; laybys, populated with whores servicing the truckers that crisscrossed this vast plain, out from Budapest, South to Serbia, East to Romania and the Ukraine, North to Slovakia and West to Austria; hoardings advertising things that seemed to have come from a galaxy far, far away – until buildings, with strange names began to appear, and before long we were in Kecskemét, and parked up outside of an old, brown, rather forbidding Communist Housing block, in Bosckai Ut, with Sandra, the outgoing teacher and occupant hanging over the balcony, yelling *"Isten hozott Kecskeméten!"* which I assumed meant Welcome.

7, Bosckai ut. My flat, top floor balcony, where Sandra hollered down!

We went up to our little flat on the top floor, at the end of the block, past the window where sat, for the entire year, a child with learning difficulties, whose eyes followed us when we passed the window, never moving, never smiling….she's probably still there…..and into a flat which probably hadn't altered since the 50s. It was like a movie set – a house in aspic. The furniture was massive, dark and ponderous and arranged in a totally impractical way. Two great single beds in the bedroom; a dreadful dark brown and orange bouclé bed – settee and a telly that had been there since Logie Baird had invented it. Sandra seemed surprised to see *two* of us, even though I had told her on the phone, but she said, *"I'll stay on for a couple of days, as long as you help me move to Pécs. Who's sleeping where?"*

"Oh, you stay in your room; we'll take the put you up for a couple of nights."

"You mean…..? Oh…. I see……."

No more was said.

We went to Pécs with her a few days later, me in the car with her and David by coach, passing a dead horse on the roadside, all four hooves pointing to the sky, which nobody had seemed to notice, helped her move in, stopped over and then returned to our new town, our new flat and our new life.

As it happened, our stuff *was* ages. It was impounded at the Austro – Hungarian border for days and we had to pay to get it back. It was all so very strange. The food, the manners, the customs, the buildings, the language – oh god, the language... It took about 3 weeks to be able to say 'a kilo of mushrooms, please' in the market. (*Egy kiló gombát, kérek*, if you must know!) but it was so liberating – after I'd got over my crippling homesickness and feeling utterly lost in this strange land. And I was, proper homesick. Why else would I pay 4000HUF, about ten quid, for a copy of The Sunday Telegraph which never arrived until the following Thursday, and fall upon it like a man possessed? Toast? I couldn't even have toast!! Bits of bread, held over the gas ring on a fork, charcoal on the outside, hot and raw in the middle, was as close as we got (although we did discover a toaster, a new-fangled foreign artefact, for sale in the supermarket. But, still in its infancy, toaster technology – there was a single strand of wire inside so you ended up with hot bread with a black stripe. And it packed up after a week and you had to get a special form before you could have it repaired and the only repair shop was miles away. We binned it. But, it was a start). But, gradually, gradually, as I got used to these wonderful polite and welcoming people, uttering strange things like *Csókolom*! (I kiss your hand!? What??) and *Jó Reggelt Kivánok!* – Good Morning, everyone! (Only around breakfast time though –after that it changed to something else) *and Viszonlátásrá*! ("Bye! See you later!") as I passed, and I was loved by my students – an exotic creature, from a strange land, far far West of here – and teaching returned to that place of wonder and joy, where people had a thirst to know and to learn….I remembered. And it was good.

Hungary had been occupied, suppressed, oppressed since 1956 – all of my lifetime! – and when the Berlin Wall fell in 1989 (a wondrous event, David Hasselhoff, notwithstanding.. of ALL the people in the world to choose from….) and the Russians finally packed up and left, the population didn't quite know what to do with itself – it had been told how and what to think for 33 years and still, in 2001, 12 years later, there was an air of disbelief, of not being sure that 'this' was allowed. Of course the people I was teaching were the new age, they were still in primary school when the Universe shifted, speaking Hungarian and Russian. A tsunami of TEFL teachers swept East, sweeping away the oppression and Russian and bringing welcome English and Kiwi fruits, received with with joy and wonder. So, I was in the vanguard, still, of this new age, teaching trainee teachers at the Uni who would qualify and then teach MY skills in the primary schools – a kind of Pyramid Selling for Nouns and Verbs. It was exhilarating, knife edge stuff dealing with students so excited by acquiring second language, being so proud, in Year one, of constructing *"Hello. My name is Gábi and I am learning to speak English so that I can teach children"* Those tenses! All agreeing! Meaning loud and clear. They loved it and so did I.

Entrance to my College.

It no longer mattered I had to use a crappy old twin tub that flooded the bathroom every time I did the washing. That I couldn't get any English telly. That all the red wine was sweet (yes, really!), that my mobile wouldn't work properly, that I was earning 1/8 of what I was before – I had enough money, plenty in fact compared to the Hungarians, whose economy was severely depressed – I was a millionaire practically, and in more ways than one. Racing, at dawn, across the Great Hungarian Plain, in a Trabant with 5 Hungarian language teachers shrieking at each other in Martian (this was September, a month after I'd landed, and I was also now working for a Language School in the city – even more money! Really – a meal out for two, with drinks? About a fiver) going to the airbase at Szolnok to teach helicopter pilots how to pass an English exam, I was struck by how utterly surreal the situation was...

.....after being searched by a fully tooled up soldier (ooh, missus!) we were allowed in to the base and I was confronted by a classroom full of 20 or so pilots, in full uniform; guys who flew helicopters in war zones, all calling me 'Sir' and looking at me with hope in their eyes that I would help them to pass. How they hated it, this requirement, how unmanned they felt, but without which there could be no promotion, but with great deference, they asked for my help to prepare their 'live talk' (I never want to hear about truffles or the assembly of a model battleship again. Ever), with good humour at their poor pronunciation and mangled sentences, constructed in such convoluted ways and so different from their Magyarul tongue, but with a fierce determination that was both impressive and humbling.....

......so far away from the life I'd known. I was asked once by one of the teachers why I had come to Hungary – nearly all the young folk were determined to leave, now that they were able – and I replied: *"For an adventure and to teach English; I'm good at it and I needed a change"*. They seemed perplexed and then asked me how much I earned 'back home'. Extrapolating it up, my old salary worked out at about SIXTEEN MIILION FORINTS a year. They were on about 400,000HUF. I worked it backwards – about 900 quid. I felt a flush of shame. And a revelation in myself. WHY did I need that? I didn't – that much is proven.

At what joy I found here! The main town square? That was designed by renowned architect, Farkas Gábor. I taught him *Angolul*. Prof. Dr. Török László, Internationally reknowned cancer specialist? I taught him *Angololul*....I was given a free ticket by a student as a thankyou, to go with her choir to Budapest to see Sir Harry Christopher and The Sixteen perform; the most generous of gifts – and just for talking to people and empowering them in a different language. I was asked to teach a Saturday morning class for adults (who needed yet another paper qualification) and it was wonderful – and at the end of the course, The Saturday Morning Gang, as they dubbed themselves, got up on the main stage and performed a play, In English – from *'Play Ten'*! Still serving me, after all these years! – those people, embarrassed and shy 12 weeks earlier, acting, up there, in front of their peers, all the other Saturday morning students, in English and just bursting with pride. As was I. Mothers, after a long day in the shop came to me, after work, to learn – *'The Leetle Preence'* was one woman's favourite story; she sat her exam FIVE TIMES, just to say to her children she had done it, that she was she was now an 'English Speaker'. Students of all abilities, all improved – not *because* of ME, though I'd like to think I played a part, but because they were able, they were free, they were motivated, thay were proud of their new skill and it was wonderful.

It was a strange and wonderful time – snow! Snow, deep and crisp and even, for *months*, a totally new experience – snow duty, to shovel clear the pavement outside our block; the coldest winter in thirty years – on New Year's Eve, in Hösök Tér, in Budapest, it was -28C – thrilling and other wordly and brilliant for keeping the champagne cold for midnight, after which we left the Square and ran back to the flat, not Heroes, where I was sick behind the radiator in Doug's spare room, and passed out. Too many pints of *sör*! Curse you, *Pálinka,* you spirit distilled by the Devil himelf! Damn you, *Unicum,* hell in a black and yet inviting bottle! Sorry Doug...

That Summer was the hottest I had ever known – up to 40C and no beaches for hundreds of miles! It was surreal to see the pavements shimmering with the heat, and people sitting in the fountain, newly built in Szabadság Tér, *'Freedom Square'*, every place name celebrating Liberty and Freedom, and after strong men who fought and died for it. Beer tents sprang up everywhere, I soon learned to order a pint or two *(Egy pohár sört kérek, a barátomnak pedig egy pohár vörösbort legyen kedve!"*....a pint of beer and a small glass of red wine, thank you very much, for my mate! (Diana, from Atlanta, who was studying voice and flute at the School) and there were free concerts in the main square, it was joyous, I was learning to let go of what I knew, and to embrace the new.

There has been much writing about matters serious, and I imagine, dear reader, you may be wondering what had happened to our jolly little homo?

Well.....nothing! Nothing doing! Hungarian men, like all races (except I suppose, the Chinese) were lovely and hairy and hnnnggggg to look at but their political freedom apparently wasn't the only thing that had been suppressed....they were so far back in the closet, they were all in Narnia. There were of course (as there always, always is) those furtive looks, holding eye contact fractionally longer than is necessary, just long enough to telegraph signals but...Well, when I say *nothing*, I meant only *once*, m'lud.

Location of the *Sör kört*...

David was back in the UK – I was working, it was term time – and the usual huge *sör kört* ('beer circle'? Never did work out why....) had been erected in the square, there was a band, of sorts, givin it some welly, and yours truly, several *pohárs* too many, (why were Hungarian pints so lethal?) was wibbling around the flower beds, pleased to be alone for once, and then.. I caught the eye of a lovely hairy bearded man, sitting alone on a bench. So, shamelessly, I went and sat next to him! Trollop! Look, this isn't going to be particularly romantic or even titillating...it was just a cock that passed in the night; or, more accurately, the evening. It wasnt even dark!! Nothing to write home about, and in fact never written about *anywhere* until here, now. The deal was struck but then the problem of *how* and *where* arose. He had no English at all, so he couldn't ask me anything and my Magyarul was still shite.

"*Szia,*" he said.

"*Szia,*" I replied.

Two 'Szia's'. Deal done.

"*Kör,*" he said, pointing to his wedding ring.

"*Erm, me too,*" I said, pointing to mine. I mean. "*Én is.*" 'Me too'. Well, as good as.

I said, *"Ház?"* House? I knew that!

"Nem itt lakom. Van esetleg egy ház, ahova mehetnénk?" 'I don't live here. You have a house?' I think that's what he said.

I hazarded a bilingual guess: *"Nem. Erm....f....um...f...felesége. Bocsánat."* 'No. Wife. Sorry'...Boy Bray! You liar! I didn't have a wife and anyway, if I DID, she was in England.

This went on for some time, me racking my addled brains for the simple vocab I had learned around 'Family' – who knew it would come in so useful? Then he said:

"You. Me. Go."

And he sort of pushed me through the crowd, out of the square and down a side street, where I sucked him off in some bushes, behind the Chinese Restaurant, as the *rendőrség* drove by in their patrol cars....

Was it romantic? No. Was it hot? Fairly, I suppose, but my *sör* goggles always made things seem a better idea than they actually were – and, as my Mother used to say *"A cock is a cock. Get it when you can"*. Well actually she didn't. I made that up. I think actually she'd be less than pleased. Still not too big for a Golden Ear Whizz…..but THAT, dear readers, was the total sum of any shenanigans for the whole year. And I didn't even know his name.

I got brand new porcelain fillings, replacing the old mercury ones I'd had as a child – perfectly done, although FUUUUUUCK!!!! THAT HURTS!!!! is the same in any language; Gabriella was very kind and did her best to ignore the weeping and flailing Englishman, bleeding all over her whites. The year passed, teaching all over the city, groups, students, adults, school children, professionals, all keen all respectful and a pleasure to be a part of their lives. Fifteen, twenty trips to Budapest, sometimes for a weekend or a day trip, sometimes with the Language school that had sent me from Barnstaple who met up three times in the year for the weekend (no shenanigans), doing the sights, claiming the City as my own. Budapest, the Paris of the East, faded, glorious, and beaten but rising will always have a place in my heart. Thank you, *thank you* to all the reiki angels that sent me there, for I know it was they, preparing the way for a new and different life.

The year sped by, its end being marked by the annual ball, put on by the Coventry House staff for...I don't know who they were, but I *DO* have an abiding memory of, after singing a song about a cabbage, in *Hungarian*, natch, watching a sea of bemused Hungarian faces wondering what the fuck they were hearing – me playing and singing '*Big Yellow Taxi*' was something they'd not *really* heard before.....you couldn't make it up. Priceless.

There was also an end of year concert for the Kodály students to which we were invited, quite an honour; the school is world famous and very prestigious and a bit of a closed shop, so we were lucky to get the chance to listen to the most hideous piano music for two hours, brilliantly, sparklingly played by these young people but, that Bartók – but, jeeez, what a bloody racket, and that Liszt isn't much better.....the flautists were wonderful as was the choir but after all that astonishingly profoundly performed music the highlight, the thing I shall always hold in my memory of that bright shining year was Stefan, from the US, sitting, at the end, on the stool, while we all sobbed –

- sobbed for the friends we'd lose, for the promises we wouldn't keep, but mostly because it was the truth, and the end and playing this song:

Another Turning Point, A fork stuck in the road

Time grabs you by the wrist, directs you where to go

So make the best of this test, and don't ask why

It's not a question, but a lesson learned in time

It's something unpredictable but in the end it's right

I hope you had the time of your life

So take the photographs, and still frames in your mind

Hang them on a shelf, in good health and good time

Tattoos of memories, and dead skin on trial

For what it's worth, it was worth all the while

It's something unpredictable

But in the end it's right

I hope you had the time of your life.

'Time of Your life'. Green Day.

The World Famous Kodály Institute

Yes, I did

In more ways that I could even know right then, sobbing and sad and grateful in the Concert Hall, Kodály Intézet - Kéttemplom Köz 1, Kesckemét, Hungary.

And on we went. .

Szerencés Mr.Lucky!

CHAPTER SIX.

NEARER TO, YET EVEN FARTHER FROM MY HOME.

In which our hero discovers bratwurst, bockwurst and, the very worst – he's in the wrong body.

'The Logical Song'.

by Scooter. No.4. August 1st, 2002

It's not a difficult question, but…can someone tell me who I am?

~ ~ ~

The end of my Hungarian adventure came quite suddenly really; retrospectively, I don't know why I made the choice I did – I was settled in this strange land, valued and solvent and I had no reason to return the UK (as long as my supply of videos of EastEnders kept coming, deliciously eked out, one every couple of days, to make them last) so…..

David was away again, and I, browsing the internet for porn and jobs (do they go together?) on TEFL.com (oh, I had completed my course by the way – with honours. I found some teaching materials the other day: I did actually know what the pluperfect was at one point…) and saw they were recruiting for TEFL/TESOL teachers in Germany. Bremen. Never heard of it, but that hadn't stopped me this time had it? I rang the number, like on autopilot….it was like being back in Enfield, 1979:

"Hello? Is that the English Language Service?"

"Yes. Hello."

"I see you are looking for staff?"

"Yes. Are you TEFL qualified?"

(Swelling a lickle) *"Why, yes. With honours, actually."*

"OK, where are you? In the UK?"

"No, Hungary."

"Oh, OK, when can you start?"

Like, don't you want to know my name, age, experience, shoe size....?

"Term is finishing here in a few weeks – I'm at the University, you know – so, maybe September?"

"OK, see you then then. Bye."

And that was that. When David rang that evening (no doubt to see if I was in) I said,

"Erm....Ive got a new job."

"Oh, where? Was it that new ifjúsági klub they were trying to get on the books?"

(If U SHAGi HAHAHAHAHAAAA Grow up Bray) *"No, not the Youth Club."* (why do you always have to be so fuckin clever?) *"Its um....in Germany. In a language school. September I start."*

SILENCE. This wasn't going too well.

"Really good money....and a flat. New experience......"

"We'll talk about it when I get back". And he hung up. How rude.

Surprisingly, when he did get back, after the usual huffing and puffing, mostly because HE hadn't made the decision, he acquiesced, admitting that it WOULD be interesting and new. We were both really sad to be leaving, but at least we weren't going back to the UK.....

The time came soon enough. Of course it wasn't only us and it was made easier because our friends were leaving too – the Kodally students (as idiot James would keep calling them) were also graduating and being dispersed back across the globe, solfege-d up to the eyeballs, so, fa, doh-ing to the children of the world (or maybe not – perhaps they all went straight home and into McDonalds..) and so many of the anchors holding us here would be weighed and so maybe it WAS time to go too….pretty hard to leave though. I had grown to love the town.

Before we knew it, all our stuff was back in in the boxes we'd saved and *en route* to Bremen, as were taken to Keleti állomás to catch the big blue train West, through the Czech republic, past Brno, past the spires of Prague, this sprawling land which would soon be under feet of water as the country suffered the worst floods for years, us watching it on the news, thinking "we were there, oh my…….", each border being checked by fully armed (delicious but scary as..) guards checking passports, glaring, through Dresden, changing trains with moments to spare and on to Berlin where we'd booked a two week break. Well, I say, 'we' – HE had booked a two week break, as if to snatch back control of the situation.

It's very strange, this period. I felt disconnected, lost – in Hungary I really felt I knew where I was, who I was but now, suddenly back in the heart of this great throbbing city I felt undone again. This is all retrospective of course and it all unravels as I write and look back on that time. Guess what? We bought some stuff!! Massive CD store, bargain bins, and there I was, like a crack whore, buying stuff I would probably never listen to….how quickly we forget….

The city was busy, it was August, we pointed, and oooh-d and ahhh-d at stuff – the Dom (utterly obscene, with homeless people on the steps outside); the Fernsehturm, with its super-duper lifts and revolving restaurant at the top, from which you could view the deprivation and acres of Communist housing from the former GDR; Ka-De-We with its glittering escalators and acres of perfumery and 'fancy goods'; *Der Deutsch Oper* with its velvet and marble and posters of the famous singers who had performed there, where we were lucky enough to get seats to see the Alvin Ailey American Dance Theatre, at €45 a pop; all of this was wonderful and I was grateful for it; the restaurants, the bars all gratefully received but it somehow felt wrong in my heart. I put it down to 12 months cultural deprivation (In all that time, the Sixteen and Sebestyén Márta were the only cultural events we'd seen.) and it felt a bit weird to have such undiluted emotional responses to wealth and opulence. Even as we strolled down Unter den Linden, I missed my unmade roads and dusty buildings where I had felt the first becomings of what I felt I truly was.

Visiting The Jewish Museum, an apparelled design by Daniel Libeskind, was powerful and more real to me than visiting the Kurfurstemndam with all its glittering shops; the small underground spaces, with empty bookshelves built under the paving stones on Bebelplatz, the *'Night of Shame'* monument to the Book Burnings that took place there on May 10, 1933 was a very visceral experience, as was the Wall, or what was left of it, painted on by people in pain and fear. The small crypt holding the statue of the mother holding her dead son while rain cried tears through the hole let in the roof was far more moving and relevant – it was pure spirit, pure grief. Checkpoint Charlie with is faded militarism and board where people stood mooning at cameras, trampling on the place where people had died, suffered, were lost.

I came to understand that this place, for all its glitz and glamour, wealth and effort, was barely concealing its past – a place of loss, and mourning, exemplified in the great grey monoliths of the Holocaust memorial, across which students and kids jumped and skittered and shouted, and the graves of 8000 Russian soldiers in Treptower Park.

But, I pressed this all down, and sightsaw and shopped, imbibed and ate like nothing was wrong. I was glad to leave. It wasn't a holiday, it was a lesson. It was my reiki helpers saying, *'Open your eyes. Look beneath…..you may not like what you see, but you must look….'*. I was unaware of any of this going on 'below'. I just felt wrong. Our two weeks staying at Willi's B+B was shall we say, adequate.

We left, and went on to Bremen.

Another four hours, via Hamburg, to my new home. Hot, hot sun, and Bremen *banhof* was packed, on this bleaching August day. And, the man who was supposed to meet us wasn't there. *Ja*. Great start. He turned up eventually and bundled us ('Us? You never mentioned 'us'?' Ooops.) and our four suitcases and guitar in to his car and then said:

"Steve. My names Steve. I own the school. You must be….?"

"Nigel. We spoke on the phone?"

This was sounding a bit weird now – it was like we weren't expected….

"Yes, I know. And this is….?"

"I'm David." That was it. No 'friend', boyfriend', 'partner' bum chum', nothing. *"Pleased to meet you."*

"Oh, and your flat's not ready. Sorry. Will be soon, though!" This was the beginning of a kind of Frank Spencer World, where nothing was quite real, ever on time, finished…..

"But, I've got you somewhere else, just temporary, until it is. I'll just have to give her a ring and tell her erm…..well, just tell her….hang on," and he dialled a number and in what appeared to be fluent German spoke to someone to tell her she had two homosexuals moving in to her house. Fortunately she was cool about it, though he wasn't, because it seemed she just increased the rent….I'm *SURE* I told you….how interesting that maybe I didn't and what did THAT mean on a subliminal level?....and so we set off around the quaint city, buzzing with Summer people to our new home.

Quite nice, I suppose. Kitchen, bedroom, lounge. Ghastly décor but…..and after a few days our stuff arrived again. This of course was a pain in the arse because there was nowhere to put it and no point in unpacking it because our proper flat was going to be ready 'soon', which actually turned out to be almost a month. So our stuff, still all boxed was crammed down a stairwell to the basement and everything was unreachable. Frau Schwimmer was very nice though we only bumped into her in the shared lobby; they lived upstairs, but as there were no shenanigans of any kind, having two homosexualists beneath her feet seemed to be no problem for her.

And so began the next phase of my journey and without sounding all whooooooo and poncy about it, I was beginning to realise that this, the travelling, the things I had seen, experienced and felt were planned, *meant*, as the journey was becoming very much an internal one. Jim had said to me, long long ago, that Reiki will find its way, do what it needs, in its own time and – DUH – I was realising that this was as much a spiritual journey as anything else. I went to the school, met the staff – all itinerant, passing through, earning enough cash to travel on; the turnover was astonishing- the whole staff must have changed 3 or 4 times during the 10 months I was there. Some were nice, some were arses, some single, some couples, some barely able to *SPEAK*

English, let alone teach it, with accents so broad even I couldn't understand them so the poor German students didn't stand a *katze* chance, and to my knowledge (and my Gaydar is usually pretty good), nobody gay. How weird is that? I was assigned some classes, often at really shitty times of the day (new boy – hurrah, thought the others) having to be out at Stahlwerke Bremen at EIGHT A.M, and the steelworks were a tram then a bus ride away. I'd expected it be full of rough tough muscly steelworkers, but alas, it was the corporate HQ, full of offices and suits (though I wasn't complaining at THAT bit), professionals who needed better English, so they could climb the corporate ladder....and get a bigger car, and a nicer office, and boss more people around....like a Deputy Head only with grownups. Hmmmmmm. Why was I here, I wonder? Most of my work was like this – a late gig, 6.30 – 8.30, at Kellogg's HQ (which took me through the cruising park. Quelle domage!), same clientele; Kraft Foods – young women striving to make it in the corporate world need English; the under managers at BMW; the buyers at AirBus who needed to go to Filton in the UK to Do Deals – all these people needing little old me! It was hard work, I have to say and the clients were particularly demanding (Lucky I knew what a pluperfect verb was, how to identify a gerund and use a past participle when asked, eh?) but, they were paying for it, it was a significant investment for the companies who funded it and Steve was very good a negotiating a good deal. Which meant too, we were paid decently. Which was just as well as we were now living in a city with all the attendant expenses – a *pohar sör* was no longer €1.20, but about €4.50, (even Beck's which was bloody well brewed in Bremen, right across the road from the flat!), eating out was dear, rent was high.....and here I was, back in the 'civilised' world. Karstadt, Kaiser, Kaufmann. H+M, all the big stores, groaning with stuff to buy. Shops, bars, restuarants, banks, commodities all yelling, yelling....It was noisy, lighty, shouty, sparkly...

Dont get me wrong, it was pretty good on the whole – the city is small, manageable with a long cultural history, lots to do and lots to see. There is also a large expat community; there's an American airbase near and the boys were often in the bars, so, unlike Hungary, language was never a problem and most of the Germans spoke, and liked to practise, English. We soon settled back in to the comfortable pattern of being consumers, and for a while after the 'difficulties' of Hungary, it felt nice, it felt deserved – we worked hard, unsociable hours so why SHOULDN'T we have a bit of a spend up.....? And yet,

yet.....it didnt feel quite like it used to. Maybe I was just out of practice? Imelda Bray needs more time.....

Why was I ignoring the reiki working away inside? Probably because it would start saying things I didn't want to hear...

...SO I set to. There was a fabulous bar just around the corner from the School, and on our way home. We had, after about 6 weeks moved into our proper flat, on the very top floor of the building in which, at street level, was Burger King which often proved most useful, staggering back form Johnny's after a few Beck's.... It was very modern and airy, with massive rooms, although getting up the78 stairs after a night on the lash was not always welcome. However, we could see the main street through town, there were tram stops right outside the door (handy for that 07.00 stumble out the door for the Steelworks gig), 5 minutes walk from school, 2 minutes from Johnnys....just perfect, except that the landlord had his office in the flat too so if we was shaggin (not that often sadly) we had to keep the noise down. A small con for a flat with a great many pros.

We found Johnny's almost right away. One lunch, after David had met me from my 10 – 12 session with the unemployed adults, who had to get a certificate to show they were serious about being employed – some resentful, but on the whole, a nice if sometimes unruly bunch, we set off to the tram to get back to Moselstrasse and watch a bit of the Commonwealth Games (and reports on the awful floods in the fields we had sped over just a few weeks earlier) and, a bit peckish when one of us noticed the awnings on what looked to be a busy bar.

'Johnny's

We went down the alley and got a table outside and the waitress (who turned out to be the owner) came out and spoke to a German couple, in German, but as I pointed out to David, with a strong Dublin accent....Really? Anyway, we were looking at the menue and she came across, said, "*Sind Sie bereit zu bestellen, meine Herren?*"

"Erm...we nicht sprechen Deutsch very gut", I said. "Boscánat...Oooh, sorry, no that's Hungarian. Erm...Spechen sie Englisch?"

"Aye, for sure," she replied. "Ai'm Irish, so I am."

"Oh. Um, OK. Well, two um... Johnny Burgers, please."

"OK, now will you be wanting to drink anything at all?"

"Ja, I mean, Yes, please. Beer for me and red wine for my...friend."

Ok, Oi'll just be a minute..." (Please now go back and read this conversation in a Dublin accent for a more authentic experience).

Not long after, she came barrelling out of the door with a tray bearing the BIGGEST burgers I had ever seen and the drinks, wobbling precariously as she came towards us, nodding to customers – *"Tschüss! "Vielen danke!", "Auf Wiedersehen"! Eine minute, bitte!"* until she got to us when she said,

"OK, fellahs, what's the craic with yous tew?"

"Oh! Well, we've just arrived really. I'm teaching at the language school and er..my friend is just erm....

"Oh, glory be! Wisht, will ye? I'll be getting me friend Jan- she just LOVES the gay boys!" and she scuttled back inside only to re-emerge with Jan, a little Welsh woman, who sat down at our table and, camp as you like, said: *"Welcome. Really. You're very welcome. Ignore her – she just an old tart. I'm the real fag hag!!"* and with that, we became firm friends. The four of us became inseparable (the husbands couldn't get a look in. Joan's, the owner of Johnny's, was just a miserable twat and Jan's couldn't speak a word of English. Fuckin GAWJJJ though. Huge, hairy, muscly – Jan was half his size but he adored her and they were a wonderful couple – he just let her get on with it). Being mates with the owner certainly had its perks – free beer was the least of it! As 'a pillar of the community', and being fluent in German, she had access to all the 'do's' and quite often we'd be invited too. We ended up at the Landlord's *Fruehschoppen*, which is a kind of breakfast piss up.

Freuschoppen, Bremen

We drank 184 miniatures that morning, before 10.00, supplied by the various pubs around town, as 'tasters'. TASTERS?? Didn't touch the sides. And Becks. Oh, yes. Becks by the stein. I won't include the photo of me wearing the pink bunny ears..... oh, alright then.....

There was something, twice a year called a *rundfahrt* (HAHAHHAAAAA FAHRT!!!.Oh, Grow Up...) which traditionally meant you just loaded up a shopping trolley with as much booze as it would hold and everyone set off round the town, stopping periodically to eat and play a game, with the intention of returning from whence you began. 'Round journey'. Do you see? As you can imagine, Bremen was littered with pissed landlords and their mates who, even though they did this twice a year and think that they'd know better, didn't quite pace themselves. The road to the *schlachte* was littered with people who, on the last leg, back along the river, on the 'slaughter', so named from where the pigs were run and butchered so the blood could easily be washed into the Weser, never quite got *rund* the *fahrt*. Better luck next year…..but it was carnage.

It went on in such a fashion for the best part of a year. Either the gang from Johnny's, or the crew from the School would hit the town and mayhem ensued. Great for the spirit, bad for the liver. It became clear to me I was 'drinking to forget' – I was ill at ease, out of joint…nothing felt quite right; indefinable yet naggingly present. I wasn't *unhappy*, I just wasn't *right*. So being on the lash, out to dinner with our Argentinian friends, at poetry readings (free bevvy) with our German fiends, down the Cellar bar with our Aussie mates all seemed a good distraction. '*Unbehaglich*' is the German – ill at ease, and uncertain as to why. Though I knew. Really, I knew. But I didn't have a clue **WHAT** to do, as that bloke in Sweet once said.

Christmas came, which we, the six of us, spent at Jan's, and we were suddenly halfway through the year. It was a lovely day, other than the fact David fell over on the icy pavement and split his head open, arriving at Jan's with his head, face and clothes covered in blood. It was warm and comforting. We went out in the evening, in to the cold and snowy night, to the Christmas Market, which was every bit as magical as you would expect – *gluhwein* and *schnitzels*, oompah bands and goose – pimpled, lederhosen clad legs, bratwurst and bockwurst, and of course the dreaded *Feuerzangenbowle* – a concoction brewed by Satan himself: a traditional German alcoholic drink for which a rum-soaked sugarloaf is set on fire and drips into mulled wine and makes you really really pissed.

The Devil's Brew.

At least it did with Joan – falling around like a ragdoll, grinning and singing – and I recognised something then, in her, the same sadness I had – the feeling of being in the wrong place.

Wurlitzer, spinning like our heads.

Later, after we had left and were back in the UK, Jan contacted us and invited us to Joan's 40th birthday – a huge surprise party, with her sisters all flying over from Ireland, and we, if could come, would make it complete. We did, flying back from Bristol, all cloak 'n dagger, hiding out at Jan and Werner's. It was a wonderful, beer stained, tear stained success and Joan had a wonderful time. The next thing we heard was that she had disappeared – had just walked away and gone back home. Just like that, leaving Johnny's, her husband and Germany all behind. That sadness that I glimpsed that night – and the fact she held my hand all the way home in the taxi from the *rundfhart* and I didn't really know why? Maybe she felt it in me too, though I was so happy that night as Gill had flown over and was staying with us and it was party time! – had maybe manifested. We'd gone and we were really very close and perhaps it had been the spur, the means by which she took a good hard look, screwed her courage to the sticking place and walked away, to happiness, to a place where she did feel right. I never heard from her again.

And neither did Jan, her dear best friend who was so lost without her. Darling, generous Jan who was killed, in the end, by those marvellous breasts – her "Fabalus Tits" , 'Fi bronnau rhyfeddol', that she'd wobbled in our faces, that she'd hidden her purse between and captivated Werner with, had turned on her and the cancer had killed her within the year.

Jan and Me in The Blarney Tavern, April 2003.

They say people drop by for a purpose and I guess, though we knew each other for such a short time, that Joan was one of those; her purpose or at least THE purpose of our meeting was to light that spark of recognition that lay hidden in the dark damp, that was always guttering into light and then being snuffed again and again. Hers burned bright, bright enough for her to be guided out. Mine was barely visible to the naked eye.

We had fun fun fun, though in Bremen! Always having a jolly at Johnny's! Some dear friends came for that New Year and we all watched in amazement when at midnight on New Year's Eve as all the blokes (while we stayed inside shrieking at both the sight and the insanity of it) went outside with the bags of fireworks they'd all brought and let them off. There. In the street. All at the same time. By hand. Rockets were screaming past the windows, exploding against shop fronts, hitting people in the nuts and the knees, holding Roman candles and bangers, jumping out of the way of the Catherine wheels that just took on lives of their own and shrieked along the street while the blokes jumped out of the way. Joan must've seen the 'WTF?????' look on our faces, as we watched our friends hilariously getting scorched, and just said, *"Oh it's traditional",* and went on her way while her husband risked his eyesight and being burned alive by fireworks that were attaching themselves to their winter coats. It was mayhem, but – it was 'traditional'! We were lucky enough to see Jan Garbarek and his band in concert; plenty of films (saw *'Iris'* , or most of it, through the Afro of the man in front who sat in front of me in an otherwise empty cinema); went the fair with Joan – up on the screamy rides with her, then down into Paddy's Pit, just 'for one', on the way home. This turned out to be the night when David came closer to violence than I'd ever seen him…..

Paddy, almost certainly not his real name, had run his bar for years, in a cellar just by the station. Of course, he and Joan were good mates (in a business warry kind of way) and as we were passing, she suggested we just popped down, as *"He'll be pleased to see us, so he will."* As it turned out, he probably was as we had 'the one', then another, and another. Their speciality was the 'Irish Flag' a large shot of fuck knows what other that it was orange, green and white (there was also the 'American Flag' that they served in Johnny's, same thing, red white and blue to make the airmen feel at home. And bilious). Anyway, the place was packed and I was having a jolly good time, thank you very much, friend of the owner of Johnnies', who was a friend of the owner of Paddy's and there were a few crafty 'housers', and oh my bleddy goodnight – were we pissed! We must have had 20? With a few Becks in between. The Flags were only €1.00, it would have been rude not to. Finally it was closing. We'd been in there for hours and we most definitely needed a taxi. We got back to Hutfilterstrasse and I (was told the next day, by a gleeful Joan) just fell out of the cab on to the pavement, unable to stand to get out. So I poured. 78 stairs later, giggling and bruised, I arrived at the door of the flat.

"What fucking time do you call this?" I wish I could've said *'You're not the boss of me,'* but a) in fact he was, b) and I was pretty much in capable of speech of any kind.

"IT'S HALF PAST FUCKING ONE! WHERE HAVE YOU BEEN??"

"Joan. Paddy…!" I managed before I started that drunk laugh thing. Which was when he grabbed me by the throat and with his fist raised at the level of my face; hissed,

"Don't you laugh. Don't you ever EVER fucking laugh at me. EVER." and he pulled back his fist but nothing happened I think mostly because he couldn't support my dead weight with one hand and I slumped to the floor, there in the hall where I passed the remainder of the night. We never spoke of this again. The next day, (luckily not 08.00 at Kraft Foods or Stahlwerke!) back to work, as if nothing had happened. Though of course for me it had. 1) I'd been out, on my own, had a laugh, got pissed, didn't care and 2) I'd been threatened with violence and, given my past history with insane Father figures, that was not a good place to have revisited. Such a small moment, such a repercussion, though it would not be felt for some time yet. The flame flickered, flared and…..subsided once more.

The year passed. The trips out to AirBus, and the daily ritual of giggling like a five year old when the driver said '*Endfhart, bitte. Endfhart*', came to an end with the completion of the contract. I was given an extra evening shift at Kellogg's – Calloo Callay – but this did in fact lead to the only bit of shenanigans that happened in all of that year (despite being desperate for Jan's Werner to pick me up, carry me away and give me a good seeing to. Which he never did.) and it all came about quite by chance. Yes it did, actually.

'Out of interest' we'd looked up 'Cruising grounds in Bremen' because there didn't seem to be any which was rather odd, given a population of some half a million people so, if Kinsey was right, 25,000 of them must be poofs. SO where did they go for their jollies? There were hardly any bars – one, '*Vater und Sohn*', which surprisingly David seemed to like (Hello!! Wakey wakey…!!), was tiny with hardly any fathers, or indeed sons. So where….?

We found a web page, in German, with a google translate which told us that, apparently you could go, in the afternoons to 'the putrid stews, near the shrups and flaps'. That sounded fun, eh, readers? Anyway, it seemed, later looking back that I had wandered through those very same shrups and flaps the night I decided to walk back home after Kellog's, instead of getting on the tram. And there were men, all ogling each other, in a really dodgy looking fashion. Not like Wanstead Flats at all! The next thing, a (I have to admit) rather beautiful blonde gentleman came up beside me on his bike and said something I didn't understand. Though the meaning was quite clear.

"Sorry…..er….ich spreche kein deutsche."

"OK, all ist good," he said and just took me by the arm and led me to what appeared to be an electricity substation (classy bird, me), pushed me against the wall, and said,

"English man. Ist good!" and got his cock out, which was already hardening. He began to undo the belt of my trousers (and dear reader, please envisage the splendour of the setting – maybe this was the putrid stews? – me in my shirt and tie and, yes, carrying my brief case which by now had seen its owner in more difficult situations that it could remember).

"*Kann ich ihn blasen?*" *"?"* he said, fumbling with my flies. *"Suck the dick, bitte?"* he said, pointing at my crotch.

"Well, erm..yes well...ok.....but..." This wasn't going to well, I couldn't get my cock out because it wouldn't cooperate. Tension? Embarrassment? Don't know, but then he gasped.

 "*Das ist ok. Du bläst MEINEN!*"" and he grabbed my head and pushed it down towards what had turned out, by now, to be a most impressive erection.

"No, but, wait, just a min...." but could say no more as I suddenly found myself with a mouthful of fat German dick.

"Ahhhhh", he said, *"Das ist gute….."*

"Grrm mmoom mmm mm" I managed when just then, a voice shouted: **"JA!! HOMOSEXUELLE!"** I understood it, as it was a little bit similar to the English….
"**JA! JA! JA!!!"**

I didn't know what was going to happen. They seemed to be shouting approval – we actually could be plainly seen from the other side of the hut thing; we weren't hidden atall! – but I was taking no chances. With a great slurpy POP! I pulled his dick out of my mouth, grabbed my gaping trousers (and my brief case) and just jumped through the hedge that edged the park, in a blind panic and fell down a bank on to the main railway line. Briefcase skittered one way, I fell on my knees, trousers round my ankles, arse in the air hoping, REALLY hoping that another train wasn't due for a few minutes….I arrived home, not having been killed by a speeding train, with a grass stains on my trousers, a hole where I'd ripped them on the stones on the track and a sprained finger.

"What happened to you?"

"Me? Oh...nothing. I fell over....on the way home. I walked. And I ...fell over...."

He just looked, and said no more.

I avoided that little park from then on, although it meant a longer way home. It didn't matter though, as things were drawing to a close there. My contract, such as it was, was coming up for renewal and the question of wanting to be away for another year arose. We decided not, after some discussion, deciding that even a year in Education was a long time, and I'd been out for two now, and that if I wanted to get a job back in the UK, I had better return before things had changed too much and I would be unable to compete in the market place (Just LISTEN to yourself, man! What the hell are you THINKING?? Why did you leave in the first place? Have you forgotten so soon...?).Looking back on this, I am tempted to say that it might not been entirely *my* decision, if you get my drift.....

Joan had opened a new pub, 'The Blarney Tavern' (nothing if not original), two doors up from Johnny's and had little time for play, as she was very busy running two businesses. After the outrageous opening do, we were able to see less and less of her and our access to events became more limited too – nothing personal, just a moving on. So our social life became somewhat truncated, it was cold, and grey and February....maybe our travelling was done? I began to look online to see what was available back in the UK and quite quickly was invited back to Cornwall, for a Deputy Head interview...so off I went, all prepped, reams of notes on the 'role of ancillary staff', 'tools for learning', 'pyramidal management' (oh fer fuck's sake......you LEFT because of all this ole bollocks!) and flew to Newquay where I was met by Jean and Mary; back to theirs for some gin and reminiscences – but not enquiry......which was odd. Anyway, the interview (two dayer!) came and went, sat anxiously by the gin, waiting for the phone to ring, to hear that they were *'really sorry, but I wasn't quite right for the post'*. Actually, I fucking well was, but there was nothing I could do about that. Even more galling was the fact that one of my ex colleagues from where I was *HER* boss, got the job. Proper stitched up, I was. Ah well, Fuck 'em. More gin, waiter!

As it turned out, within weeks the head had gone off sick on long term leave and the job had suddenly become Acting Head of a Failing School which OFSTED had put into 'Special Measures'. *LUCKY* Mr. Lucky!

It had been arranged that Gill would come to visit again, reluctantly, as she was afeared of flying but…! Have no fear! I had booked myself on the same flight back and crept up on her at the airport. *"BOO!"* I said. She was astonished / thrilled / relieved and we had a jolly ginandtoniced flight back and an even more jolly week, during which David quite clearly remembered why it wasn't a good idea putting us together…..it was nice to have someone to play with, have japes instead of just being…watched. And well behaved.

So, Gill went home, and soon we were going home too. April we left, alone, in the rain, taken to the airport by our landlord (with whom I very nearly had sex with once - a final 'Huzzah'!…we were packed and ready to go, David was at the school and Bruno and I were alone in the flat, side by side looking at a painting on the wall and our little fingers brushed together – insistent, not an accident, and there was that moment of suspension when it could've gone either way. – A bit like a cottaging, but without the partition and he didn't pass me a note written in biro. In the end, he bottled it. Shame – nice hairy older man. One that got away) and soon we were in the air, homeward bound, back to Bodmin, unemployed, uncertain as to what would happen next. Tired of travelling, tired of feeling I belonged nowhere.

There was no feeling, for me, of a happy return to the land of my birth, to the Land of the Gods – I was, rather, *Unbehaglich* – uneasy, out of joint and I was increasingly aware that I was going to have soon grow a pair and face up to what was becoming inevitable. My feelings of being in the wrong life were crystallising and it would be the empty space I was now flying back to that would finally allow the reiki, the power so long stored, to come bursting forth annd ensure my real work would begin. There would be no stopping it, and no turning back.

CHAPTER SEVEN.

TREADING WATER.

Where our hero meets Michael (who'd been patiently waiting), faces the truth and finds you really *really* can't go back....

'Beautiful'.

by Christine Aguilera. No.17. April 15th, 2003

I will not be belittled. I am beautiful. I have worth. Fuck off.

~ ~ ~

So, we walk in and it's like walking into a squat. The last straw really. At least, I thought I'd have my house to go back to but the family to whom the agency had let it to had fucked off without paying rent and left the place like a, well a squat. It stank of fags and cat piss. It clearly hadn't been cleaned for – well probably hadn't been cleaned at all. There were drifts of animal hair piled up along the skirting boards, black greasy hands prints on the doors and walls. The 'recycling' was just outside the kitchen window and it reeked. It was heart-breaking. The agency, to whom we paid £200 a month to manage the house, to deal with the rent, clearly had been nowhere near the place and we'd been too far away to know. Not a propitious start, I think you'll agree. But *'somebody, somebody, up there likes me'*, as David Bowie once said (not about me obviously).

My Dad – remember him? Two years of not having to see him or deal with his Machiavellian shit; it had been most welcome – he'd decided to sell the house where Mum had died some years back and had moved into Newquay, across the road from Barrie and Rosemary. What they'd thought of this is unrecorded but I imagine Barrie said something like: Him: *"That's fantastic. He IS my Dad."* and her: *"Oh for FUCK'S SAKE. I really don't want to have to put up with the miserable old cunt living next door practically, and being over here all the time, moaning about everything and everyone."* I'd have been with her on that one. After some time he then decided to sell – sorry GIFT - that house, split the money between we five (including multi-millionaire brother Michael...) and we ended up with a lump sum each. He eventually ended up in a sheltered flat in Truro, overlooking the Cathedral. The lucky bastard.

So.

Sandra spent all hers on some failing business she and her latest fool had got themselves into.

Gill lent her £15,000 of hers to prop up said business, against everyone's advice. Business went bust. Gill never got a penny back. Massive split in the family, which had never healed to this day.

Barrie probably put his in the bank and Michael probably never even noticed.

And I, used mine to remodel my house. New kitchen, new furniture, decorated throughout, new this, new that, new Stuff. When what I should have done, while I had the money and the chance, is fucked right off, and when I got there, kept fucking off. But I didn't. We just paid some debts and it, and my chance of escape, was gone.

We now, suddenly had no income, apart from David's benefits, and a mortgage to pay. Welcome to the real world. The world I had fled from……are you just not listening? Although, to be practical, I had to go to work again. In schools as it was the only toolkit I had.

….Angels flapping their wings in frustration….

And so I applied to be accepted on the supply pool, so I could be back in the classroom! Brilliant. It was the only thing I was good at and we needed food and of course we had to start buying some Stuff again. How quickly we resumed normal service…

I got quite a lot of work actually. Some very good – more permanent, half terms, or a few consecutive weeks which at least gave you a chance to learn the kid's names and for them to learn to stop fucking about because I would be back the next day. And the next. Those were the best gigs. The one day covers were the worst…nothing was ever achieved, the kids were uninspired and disengaged and often bore a striking resemblance to those kids, so long ago, back in the Dockland School. One class, post – SATs, Summer holidays approaching, school play over (Do it the *last week*, people.....) were so bored, so difficult, that in the middle of the Maths lesson I had been left to teach (what was she THINKNG??) I slammed shut the text book, packed up my stuff, closed my briefcase and walked out.

"Where you going sir?"

"Home."

"But what about the Maths Sir?"

"I couldn't give a shit, to be honest." (Not very professional I know, but I'm a teacher, not a zookeeper and I had had ENOUGH of the little bastards.) *"Do what you fucking like."*

Passing the reception, I tossed by security badge through the hatch, said, *"You can tell the Head I've gone. Year 6 are alone. I deserve better."* And walked out. Probably never to be employed again. Actually, about a week later I received an envelope containing 36 letters of apology, obviously written under duress and therefore meaningless. I binned them.

But there WERE some great times, one in particular, which was how it USED to be – spontaneous, engaging. The head, a formidable but adored woman had called a meeting for all the staff, 'just during assembly, ten minutes at the most...'

"No worries," I said. *"I can do a song with them."*

"It's the whole school today, Friday."

"Oh. Well, no..OK, it'll be fine."

And it was! Bloody marvellous in fact. The meeting dragged on for almost 40 minutes, but when Jane hurried in, full of apologies, she was met by a wall of sound – her whole school singing a four part round and just loving it. When they'd finished, she said, *"Well children, that was wonderful! Let's all thank Mr Bray!"* and they applauded, with real enthusiasm and it felt great. Then one of the Y6 girls put up her hand and said,

"Miss, can we sing you the others?"

And Jane, seeing this for the perfect moment it was, got a chair, and sat right at the front and listened, astonished, to her school, all of them, singing songs in 4 parts that half an hour ago, they'd never even heard. All of them – the lazy, the naughty, the usually disinterested, loving the feeling that only unison singing can give. That was the highlight of all of that time and I look back on it with fondness.

One other incident of note – have you noticed how few there are? How little to tell you? When you consider the early parts of this book – always stuff going on. Now? Not a lot. What had happened to me? *Meeting David* had, that's what. And I had let it happen - concerns an old Object of Desire....I had a few days booked in at school on the South Coast and my route to it took me past a newly developed block of apartments; chic des.res. places (in one of the worst places imaginable other than it was near a massive tourist attraction), developed by none other than Steve, my nemesis, my oldest friend and still, burning bright in my memory from 30 years earlier, the most beautiful man I knew. Anyway, one of the times, coming home from school, I saw the front door open and on the spur of (premeditated - who am I kidding?) the moment, pulled in and knocked. And there he was, all business like, Suit and red tie blazing, with those eyes from which there never an escape.

"Oh. Hi!"

"Hi! (There they were again.) *I was just passing and saw your car. I thought you could show me round your 'project'? You keep going on about how good it is to people, so….."*

"Yep, come on in."

I have to say he'd done a fantastic job but then having seen his house, it was always going to be very upmarket – we went in to the lounge of the first flat and sat.

"Well….I have to admit you've done a great job here. Very nice."

A small smile played across his face. "*Yeah, its brilliant isn't it?"*

Still such an arrogant twat….but he was right. The boy'd done good.

"Let me show you round. Kitchen – sorry about the mess – we had a party here last night; I'm here trying to clear up….Bathroom…..two bedrooms, very well appointed I think you'll agree…Nice size.." What are you, a fuckin Estate agent now? I don't want to buy one, I'm just here for….well, what? What WAS I here for? We both knew of course and he was just playing me, like he always had.

Back in the lounge, sitting facing each other.

"Well there you go. They're all the same, so there's no point in going around them. Anything else you want to see?"

And there it was – that great space, that great silence we both knew would come, into which like a junkie, unable not to, I said: *"Your cock, please."* Just like that. Ooooft.

Again, that slight shimmer of a smile, like he knew this was going to happen, like he'd just been waiting…*"Bedroom Two, I think,"* and off we went.

It was like being 19 again, trembly and full of guilt and screaming passion. Hand on arm. Hand on face. Pull in to kiss, brush against rough face, hand on belly, fingers on shirt buttons, hair, oh! Sweet Jesus! that belly hair, belt buckles clicking, trousers falling, cocks straining, pulling together feeling the thrust and heat of erections…and a great silence, a stillness that echoed back down the years to London, to Chris, to the agony this man had caused me and with that fleeting rush of thought, my ability to perform this ritual was over. My erection wilted and I felt foolish and ashamed.

"Hey. What's up? Don't you fancy me anymore?" He was holding his cock, proudly jutting out from that impossible riot of hair, dark strong legs, full balls, belly hair – like a photograph, like the most beautiful thing, in aspic.

"No. I mean, yes of course…I don't know what happened. Give me a minute…." and standing in the bathroom, looking at my shrivelled dick, I knew this was a huge mistake and I just didn't know why I was even here. …..Actually, yes I did. I did actually. It was to prove that I had a life outside of my tiny room. Being able to make a decision, to do something spontaneous, to do something I wanted, without having to ask….to prove that I still had a life of my own….even if it was to cheat on my lover.

I looked into the bedroom and he was now on the bed, in the falling light, his cock hard and proud and he was still beautiful, still capable of inflaming a rage of lust and with that thought, I responded and joined him on the bed. Running my hand across that glorious spread of hair on his chest, down his belly, down the dark trail to his beautiful cock, cupping his balls tenderly……it *WAS* déjà vu, but beautifully so, and, knowing this, I was healed – that sadness, residual in my heart from so long ago, left me with a soft whisper; I didn't even know I was carrying it but there it was, and now it was gone.

"Can I fuck you?" he said.

"No, it's too personal for me. Too symbolic, too…. we're not lovers, so for me it's a bit too much."

"You didn't used to be so fussy…"

"Ah. But then, I loved you, then I thought we were lovers, **then**, I thought that we were, we would be….."

Oh, OK, well, just suck me off then." Nothing if not pragmatic…..

Which with great alacrity and joy, I did, knowing as I took his cock in my mouth and as I tasted the salt of his sperm, it was like a benediction and I knew for certain, that this would never happen again. It was done. Just like it had been with my other drug, Rod, back in Ilford – the last hurrah. I didn't know how heavy they'd been until they flew away.

So here we were, back in the world I'd left behind. Going out to the curry house – *'there's nothing like an English curry! They're shit in Germany….'* – and the kebab shop. Clothes. CDs. Stuff. Shoes. Stuff. Bigger better telly. Stuff. It all felt so wrong, like I had had an out of body experience. You know, like in those films where the action freezes for ages – days, months, years even – and then starts off again exactly in the same place? Well, that's what it was like. It was like I'd been abducted by aliens for two years and it all went on, same old, same old and then I just reappeared and it seemed nobody had noticed I had gone! I don't recall being asked, not once, about my adventures; not one single *'ooh what was it like in Budapest? 'What did you do in Germany?'*….it was a feeling of dislocation, being back in a world that SEEMED the same, and fact was, very much so, but I was different. I'm not saying I'd *'moved on'*, *'improved'*, become *'better'*; just that I didn't fit anymore, I was on the edges, looking in.

Sure, people were pleased to see us at parties, when we went, but it was the same old thing, the same group, the same conversations, as if I'd just nipped out for a two year fag break. Don't get me wrong – I loved these people, they were my friends and I had known them many years, but now….and I only know this now as I look back and try to unravel all the events that led me down the path I took later…but now, there seemed to be a….a sheet of glass between me and them; very thin so I could hear everything, see clearly, but not quite be in touch.

So…what was this telling me? Probably that I was the world's worst Reiki Master who couldn't tell his angelic realm from his arse. Why didn't I connect these two things? I was being guided, guided away to a new place, nudged gently by spirit and I just kept buying CDs! Brilliant.

On our return however I have to say that meeting up again with Anna was a significant thing – she was and always has been an old soul, able to see through most of the bullshit of this world, including mine, so when she said, *"Why haven't you started your healing practice yet?"* I was both flummoxed and busted at the same time.

"You were sent away so you could shake off this life, and find a space to begin a new one. Spirit has been yelling, so loud, I could hear it, and you just keep turning up the volume on the CD player drowning it out. What are you so scared of? Of course, you can chose what you want – that's part of the deal, but really, should you be wasting time and NOT beginning? You will be a very powerful healer, if you don't let you ego get in the way. Now go. Make a difference". I'd been busted and bollocked. All at the same time.

What I was scared of was being shit at it. It was all very well 'doin' yer mates', but asking people to pay for something *SO* intangible was a difficult thing for me to reason. The energy, the chi, the Universal Force was free, so it just didn't feel right to ask for money. David's *"Well, you could get the £450 back that I paid for the training"* aside, there was something about people paying for a service and I guess giving reiki was that, albeit a mighty life changing one. Actually….put that way, it was worth every penny – so, armed with a somewhat shaky reasoning, I bought a couch and began to advertise and…LO! They came. *'Build it and they will come'*, as Kevin Costner once said, and it seemed as if everyone had been waiting for me (or more accurately, someone who could give them reiki) and I soon built up a small, but regular client base. What this also did was to move me further still, away from the life I had had before. As I tuned into spirit more and more I became reluctant to be buying stuff I didn't need - shopping became something about which I felt increasingly guilty, but conflicted because I still had another life, one which involved parties and restaurants and needing clothes for them, and maybe a different cologne. (I didn't! Of course I didn't, but undoing so many years of habit is not easy, so don't be too hard on me - I was doing my best, with Michael's help.) Oh, let me introduce you – Michael, these are my lovely readers who have been with me for some time now (about 374 pages and 47 years); Readers, this is Michael. He is an archangel. He is the one to whom I have been assigned for guidance and when healing, he's the one who comes and shows me what to do. Nice wings, eh?

There is a third strand running along in this interlude in my life, where I was between lives, and one that also had an effect on what happened later. When we came back, we had a new neighbour. Well, she'd been there before we left actually, but David thought she was 'hippy' and beneath us, so we never spoke to her (I didn't seem to have much choice – I thought she looked pretty cool, but…..well, you know.) But when we came back, she and I made a real, deep connection, on two levels: she was deeply spiritual and connected with the Earth, its fairies and its plants, and, she was a total pisshead. We got on very well, and by now, somewhat more independent, I began to spend a lot of time with her, next door, laughing, smoking roll ups and sometimes joints (the first drugs I'd had since that heroin I had back in Clapham, in the late 70s, when I was still with Julie but fucking my mate while his sister, a high class escort was out earning thousands of pounds and being dined (but not fucked) by rich Arab business men……

…I have just realised that I hadn't quite mentioned any of this! OK. My bad. I have thought hard about this episode, quite forgotten, and I cannot remember for the life of me where I met him….it MAY have been Harrods, it might have been…..no wait! I think it was Slobbidybobbidy who met his sister, and she invited us to their magnificent house on the edge of Clapham Common. That must be it – I cannot think of any other way, or place. Her brother Steve, or Deemo was there, as he preferred to be called and he was obviously gay and not my type at all, and anyway, I had a girlfriend blah blah…..thin, hawkish, no body hair (I didn't know yet what hankie he would've worn, as at that point I hadn't been 'educated' by Chris in the Salisbury, but as it turns out, it would have been Navy blue, and worn on both sides. FYI.)

Anyway, dinner was very grand; mostly because Fran worked as a high class escort and the night before, one of her regulars had given her a ruby ring and two grand. This was the late 70s remember. That was a fucking fortune! So, we had my very first lobster, and good (apparently) champagne. We all got completely pissed, Julie crashed, and I ended up fucking Deems. And the other was round. It was nice. Unexpected, and it didn't mean anything cos I had a girlfriend etc. I KNOW what you're thinking….but the Cock Imperative + Champagne = Inevitable Shagging. Many of you would have done, have done, the same. Thing was though, I kind of had a little thing for this sweet unsuitable man and went to see him quite often – *"Just going over to Clapham, be back late. Love you.."* – how it was ever entertained I don't know; sometimes she came with me and, dear readers (OK, now this IS bad) we used to get really pissed and go to bed and then I'd get up when she'd fallen asleep, creep down and shag Deemo, who would always be waiting. Or the other way round. Or one after the other. It was a very odd thing. We'd go to the Two Brewers on the High Street, a notorious gay pub, and somehow it was alright. The more I write this the more I realise what a transition period this was. Before, the 'I have a girlfriend' stuff only applied at Balls Park (BALLS Park HAHAHHAAA!) and we had already been through the Tony debacle and were now in our little love nest in Leyton. Only clearly it wasn't THAT cosy. We had a nice time – it was like *being* gay but not really, because …yeah, yeah. Fooling nobody, least of all Julie. This was clearly the chrysalis stage; I was pupating in Clapham. Anyway, that set the scene for this bizarre interval of time; it couldn't have gone on for more than a few months because in 1980, I'd moved out, Chris had come to London and it had all gone a bit Pete Tong, as they say. So it must have been May 1979. I know that, because I was at Deemo's and Fran came home, after a night shift, clutching a bag and contained therein was David Bowie's *'Lodger'* album which was just released on May 18th and she had bought it instantly (cash probably, as she'd made about £800 that night – *"He's not one of the generous ones",* she'd say, waving around a wad of money it'd take me a month to earn. *"Dinner was nice though, and I did get this necklace…"* and put it on the record player and *'Fantastic Voyage'* filled the flat, with Bowie's extraordinary voice soaring through the flat and making her wee a bit. After we had some dinner, and as Talking Heads' *'Fear Of Music'* was put on the system in the lounge, this happened:

"I've got some coke, if you want some." said Fran.

"No, I'll stick with the beer thanks," I said.

"No, you tart Coke. COCAINE," said Deemo.

"Oh. Erm….."

"I'll have a line, Fran," he said and cut it on the black and green album cover. I watched in fascination. I KNEW about it of course, but had never seen it. I felt very cool indeed. After two or three more beers, I was feeling rather less inhibited so when Deems said, *"Can I have another line, Fran?"* I said, *"Me too, please!"*

"None left. He only had a bit. Got some heroin though."

And yes, somehow, they persuaded me. I wasn't injecting it in to my eyeballs or anything, before you all gasp. It was tablet form and anyway they and the beer said it would be OK, so, to the sounds of 'I ZIMBRA' I took my first (and only) heroin. I don't know what I was expecting, actually. But, if you try to listen to the lyric of the last track on that album, *'Drugs'*, you may get some idea.

It was fuzzy, it was rushy, it was hot, it was peculiar, it was loving......I've never had it since, although I would've then, in an instant, but they of course refused. Anyway – there you go. May '79 until 2003 – completely clean! I don't know what happened to little Deems. We lost touch gradually – it was one of those strange interludes, strangers colliding, moving through. For me, it was another brick on the tower of homobricks that I was, at that time, valiantly trying to balance, the weight of which was becoming unmanageable.

So, my neighbour. The third of the Three Tall Women, sent to make David's life unbearable.... Gill, which bond he could never break; Ann, who was too wise to be daunted and Gaynor, who really didn't give a shit what he thought. His unholy Trinity. But I loved (and still do) love them all and each brought something to my table: love, courage and joy. Some of each from each of them.

The Triangle of

Healing.

Making my Body a temple, practising my reiki and trying to make things better through love and light.

Escaping.

Drink vats of wine, smoking dope, get pissed and be a child again.

Drowning

Try to fit back into the real world, shop, cook, teach, iron, pretending nothing had happened.

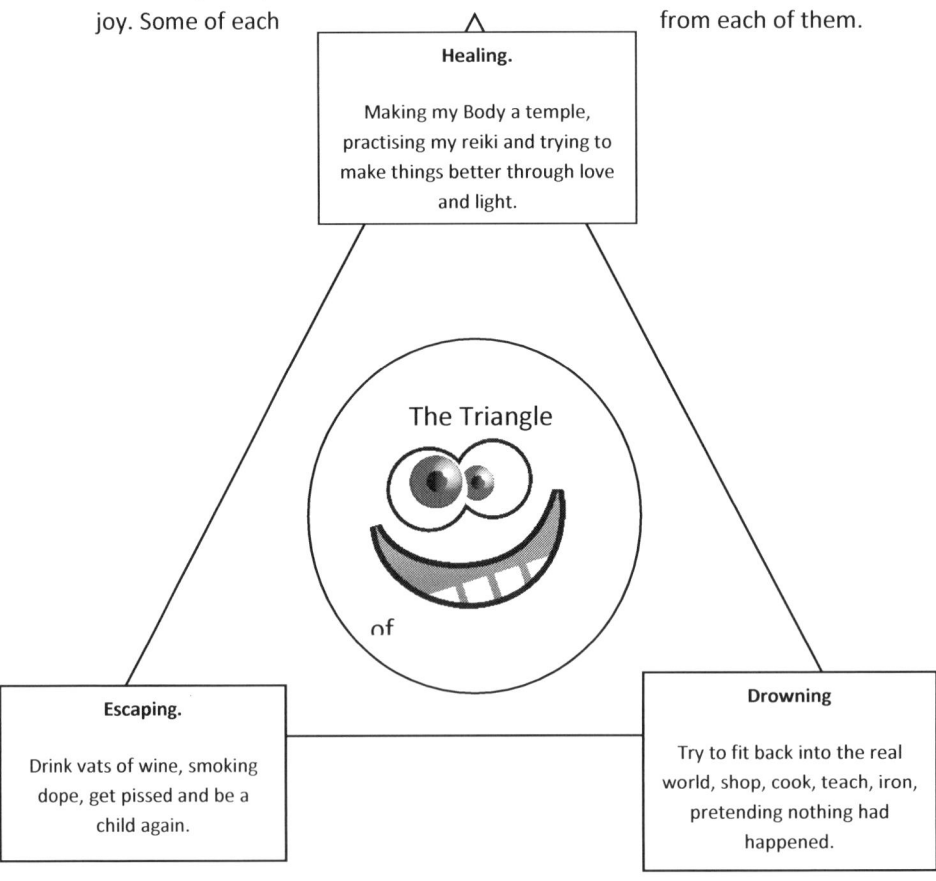

Mr. Lucky's Triangle Of Confusion.

I had no bloody idea where I was. I careened from corner to corner of this triangle, never settling, at each point feeling that I should be at one of the other two. It was madness and I felt really really lost. In addition to all this – between setting up my practice (ignoring Michael tutting and flapping his wings in impatience), trying to get a Normal Life, like it was, in the Old Days, where nobody had any curiosity, just carried on as normal – same houses, same parties, same shops, same sex, and nipping next door for some wine a bit of weed and a mad half hour / afternoon / all dayer, I also wasn't feeling especially well. Just knackered. Verk, as we say. I put it down to too much excitement! Parties, boozing, going next door too much….I was getting on a bit you know – couldn't do it like I used to…..

And so the year passed.

How did I go from Kecskemét hero to Bodmin zero so fast?

Looking a bit desperate here…..

CHAPTER EIGHT.

MR. LUCKY IS WELL AND TRULY FUCKED.

<u>In which our hero gets somewhat of a shock, gets to pay his dues, forgets what size shoes he takes and find out who his friends really are.</u>

'Comfortably Numb'

The Scissor Sisters. No.94. 11 November 2004.

My world shattered. I was numb and dumb and all apart.

~ ~ ~

11.11.11

What does that mean to most of us? Armistice, probably. The end of slaughter. Our boys, the ones that were left, coming home with varying amounts of limbs but still coming home. The memory of war. Poppies. Everyone in black. Mourning. Loss. One war ended.

Well, for me, apart from being the old man's birthday (Oh! The irony!), it was the day, in 2004, I was told I was HIV positive.

11.11.11. My war began that day.

Mr. Lucky was, as my sainted lady mother was wont to say, shit outa luck.

Let me take you back…..

1980. Met Rod. Faithful (ish). Met Ken. Faithful. Moved back home to Cornwall. Met David. Faithful (apart from a couple of mutual wanks here and there) for 18 years. So. I know, having met Rod since, he was not infected. Ken is alive and well, and although I don't know his status, I DO know, that as a very scared ex-Jehovah's Witness, I was the first person he'd fucked. And David, as it turns out is one of the blessed few that carries the gene which prevents HIV from attaching itself and so he cannot become infected. Therefore, this puts the date of my infection somewhere before 1980, those few months of glorious sex when I had left Julie and was putting myself about a bit. It MUST'VE been then. The freedom, you see – I was able to be me, a gay man, a walking erection, a thirst for identity. But oh, what bad luck was mine – AIDS, as it was, all lilies, falling tombstones and BIG CAPITAL LETTERS, was barely in the country then, or at least not amongst the people I knew. Clearly I was wrong.

Looking back through wiser eyes, I know *now* that I was **POZ** – look at those three letters, standing out from the crowd, with no other meaning! – for TWENTY FOUR years, without knowing, having unprotected sex with David (lucky for CCR5,eh?). POZ when I lived in Leytonstone, POZ when I lived in Walthamstow, POZ when I lived in Bodmin for 17 years, POZ when I was in Hungary, POZ when I was in Germany, POZ while I was teaching….who knew eh? I didn't, that's for sure.

So, you can imagine my horror, gentle reader, that morning on Armistice Day 2004 when the kind nurse said, *"We've got your results…..and I'm afraid to tell you that they're positive…."*

"HA!" I hear you cry! *"What did you expect? We've read about your shenanigans! We know you were shagging in woods/cubicles/cars/junkshops/stranger's beds…..what did you expect? No more than you deserve, I say…."*

But, no. Nobody *deserves* this. Not the sexually active, not the queers or the hetties, not the mainliners, not the whores, not the unwilling wives of African men, not the haemophiliacs, not the trauma victims needing blood. Nobody DESERVES it. Like cancer, it has no heart or soul, no freedom of will. It is just a lickle bitty virus that some folks get – and yes, even straight ones – and their life choices or otherwise are irrelevant. It takes one needle from thousands; one fuck amongst many. You throw your hat in the ring and hope. Could've been a bus. At least you wouldn't have judged me then, eh?

"We are the product of our choices and those choices do not render us more or less deserving of love. Love me because I am human. Love me because I am flawed and made mistakes. Love me anyway even if you disagree with my choices", says Dr. Rick Coons, an American Clinical Psychologist. Just be nice, eh? It's hard enough as it is without you thinking I'm bad.

Anyway…..

There then followed a thousand year silence. I don't remember much about it actually, other than saying, *"But that's impossible. You must be wrong."* in a very tiny voice, but knowing, judging by the looks of concern from the ring of nurses looking down on me, that they weren't. But how? HOW? I hadn't had sex with anyone else for seventeen years, and yet, and yet….I'd been feeling pretty shitty on and off for quite a while. Nothing definable, just a bit verk. Looking back at my old passport photo, which I'd had to have for Hungary, I can see, now, a ghostly pallor, a kind of sickness….nothing obvious, just...well, as I said, verk. Unknown to me of course, the virus was multiplying and killing me softly, with its deadly song. Apparently, as I found out later, I was a 'long term progressor', which means I had been infected long ago but the virus had been dormant for years and years. Why it begins its march toward victory and death is not known, but for me it was my salvation. Had I 'converted' earlier, joined the church of the dying and the damned, I would have been given AZT which would have killed me sooner. As it was 2004 by now, the treatment and medication was exponentially improved and so, I was saved from the horror of cancers, blindness, dementia and death. For now, anyway.

Thinking about it now, I had had a peculiar incident the April before this, which went unresolved. I was sitting in bed at home one morning, naked, as always and David said. *"What's that?" "What? Where?"* I answered. *"There. On your chest. Oooh. And on your arms…."* Fuck! What the hell…..? As I watched, this rash appeared, as if someone was flicking pink paint. It just spread and spread, like a speeded up film until, within a few minutes I looked like Leopard Man, only pink. What the….?

David rang our doctor who, clearly puzzled and concerned, rang for an ambulance and before I knew it, I was in hospital, being stared at and prodded with a biro. No one seemed to have any idea of what it could be and stranger, I felt perfectly well - no fever, nothing. They went away, obviously puzzled having asked me the statutory list of questions. They hadn't come across the Amazing Leopard Man before and clearly weren't too clear on being anywhere near me. Maybe THEY'D catch it…..

I know now that I was 'seroconverting'; that is, that after nearly two decades of lying dormant within, something had caused the virus to break out. Having no other answer, the consultant said "HAVE AN HIV TEST". Yes, in that voice, in those capital letters, but clearly as I couldn't possibly have HIV, I told her to fuck off. Well, not quite, but obviously such a thing would have been pointless, wouldn't it?

From that time though, I began contracting odd illnesses; nothing serious but frequent. I kept going to see my doctor (for whom grateful thanks – when the ghastly truth came out, she was nothing but gentle and kind, and in the world of terror and disease I now suddenly found myself, her gentle voice and her helpful manner was of incalculable value) who kept coming up with no answer.

That day, that dreadful day, when I heard the nurse say, "YOU'VE GOT AIDS AND YOU'RE GOING TO DIE!!!!!" was a life – changer, in more ways than one. Snippets, little pieces of fragmented memories, come back when I recall that day. The consultant to whom I had been assigned (and again, whose manner and skill were to be the saving of me. Literally.) said, I remember: *" I know this must be a shock, but we can get you on the right drugs and soon you'll be saying to yourself - I have hazel eyes, I have size 8 feet. Oh and I have HIV. It will become that normal"*. I just stared at her. How could it EVER become normal? I was diseased, full of worms and death. How would it be NORMAL??? I didn't reply; I was just battered into silence by the voices in my head. *How did I have this …this **THING**? What will I tell my family? Who will ever speak to me again once they know? How much longer do I have to live? DON'T fucking lie to me!! I've seen it. I've been at the bedsides of the blind, the cancerous, the dementing, ones, as the virus dissolved their brains I was with Chris as he choked on his own body fluids .I KNOW. I KNOW. Just tell me. ……*

11 / 11. At 11 a.m. as well. Ha! That's funny eh? My world spun away from me that day. I don't recall what David said or did. He was probably horrified too, both for me and what the implications were for him, unknowing then about his charmed life

I was then whisked off in to the innards of the building, following the white coats dumbly. They sat me down and smiled and took some more blood and smiled and took my blood pressure, smiling, smiling, smiling as if that would make all better. Nothing, NOTHING was going to make this better. My sense of horror and my sense of fear and my sense of shock and my sense of bewilderment alternated, phased in and out while I just sat, motionless, speechless and tearless. How did she know I had size 8 feet? Maybe it was just a metaphor…..or an analogy. The walls were a pleasant colour. Her hands were a bit cold, the cuff a bit tight, the vein blue and pulsing, my bladder full (just as well as they wanted my piss as well as my blood and my soul).

And so it went.

We went home, numb, voiceless, to a future I was certain would be short, full of fear as to which of the sicknesses would do for me….Karposi's Sarcoma? Dementia? PCP? That's what killed my best friend, I saw it. (Oh I knew all the names from my buddying days, days when it was nothing to do with me and I could hold hands in safety). Who would be there to hold MY hand as I drowned in despair and disease? No one must know. Maybe my Dad was right? This is my punishment for joining the Shit Shover's Union.

I don't really remember the next few weeks linearly; they just consisted of countless trips backwards and forward to the clinic, where I just sat and listened, sure that it was all a waste of time. I KNEW the score, both figuratively and literally. I knew all about CD4s and CD8s, viral loads and HDL. I had been on the internet all through the nights when I was unable to sleep, trying to find answers to how long I could expect to live and how to limit the horrors of what was surely to come, neither of which, of course was possible. 25 miles one way, 25 the other, over and over.

This memoir was supposed to be a light hearted romp through my life, but gentle reader, for now, you will find no laughter here, no anecdotes, no joy. Fear, and shame. Nothing more.

I <u>KNEW</u> that there were drugs available to me and I also knew the side effects – constant diarrhoea, vomiting, nausea, weight (and cholesterol) gain, lipodystrophy, Buffalo Humps, 'Sculptra' to fill in the pits in your face and your arse, 'The AIDS Face', which would mean be being pointed at in the street, spat at like my dear dead friends were and beaten up. Lots to look forward to...

....but as my CD4 count was THIRTY ONE, and yours is probably 700, 800 and it is recommended that therapy should start when your count has fallen to 350, I was right up shit street.....the only variable really was *when* to begin the drugs. My consultant gave me good advice, but somehow I was scared, more scared of the drugs than what would inevitably happen if I DIDN'T take them. The final process was that she would prescribe them and I could take them "when I was ready". When was that going to be? Now? Next month when I was even sicker? Sometime in the future when I had summoned up the courage to face the awful consequences of putting these massively toxic chemicals into my body? Once a day. For ever – however long THAT might be.

OK, so here's the thing. On November 10th, I was OK. Not very well, but OK. 24 hours later, I knew I had AIDS. Not just HIV, but AIDS. That kills you. Well, the stuff you can no longer fight *kills* you. Just capital letters – same shit.

What a difference a day makes; 24 little hours.....it was, I don't know now, maybe a week before I began my HAART. And having AIDS brought far more with it than a compromised immune system. It brought fear and shame and stigma and shunning and loneliness and eventually a descent into a possible pain filled and messy death. And I HAD IT! Whoop whoop! What a turn up! Oh, *LUCKY* Mr. Lucky. Everyone I had befriended and nursed and comforted when I worked at the respite centre had died, more or less, as the years went by, so it seemed fairly likely that I would do. Bollocks. Bollocks. **BOLLOCKS.** This was NOT in the plan.

So. I sat on the edge of the bed, holding the pills in my hand – 3 for the HIV (only one now. Ain't science amazing?), 1 to combat the sickness I would feel, 1 to combat the diarrhoea I would get and one for the little boy who lives down the lane. They were all lovely different colours too – that would make it all much easier, much more fun. I sat on the bed. And I sat on the bed some more, knowing that from the moment those three tablets passed through my throat, that there would be no going back – I didn't know what side effects I would suffer, but I finally saw I had no choice – the virus would continue to devour me, with less and less to defend myself and eventually – quite soon, if the subliminal messages from my consultant were being correctly read – it would overrun me and I would die. Simples.

But. BUT!! And here IS some joy in this dark chapter – I had NO side effects! None whatsoever! Well, except, and I remember this clearly, much to the amusement of Nicki, that the one psychoactive episode I DID have from the Tenofovir, was that I dreamed I married Beyoncé. Really. That's all. No nausea, no squits, no humps or wasting of fat. I knew these things, if they WERE to happen, would not be immediate, but I was relieved enough just to wake up the next day.

After a week I had my next appointment (someone was sitting in MY seat, cheeky bastard. I should've had a plaque put there), I had blood results and my viral load, which had been immeasurable as the detector only went up to 1 million, had dropped to 2,038 and my CD4 had 'leapt' up to 115! In a week. In a FUCKING WEEK!!! Oh *YES*! Maybe I wouldn't die? The drugs DO work, Verve! They fucking well DO!!!! Euphoria! We all had a little dance, and a group hug, the blood nurse and me, with Nicki happy as it seemed I was responding and she wasn't going to lose me after all. We grew very fond of each other actually and it was quite hard to say goodbye when eventually I left her care.

I was so chuffed (the understatement of the century) that momentarily I forgot the reality of my situation, which was although these Wonder Drugs (they certainly WERE Highly Active!) would probably reverse my AIDS, I would still have HIV, and would ALWAYS have HIV. Dealing with that, at this point wasn't a priority. Manana. Dreckly. For now, I was going to live.

How did I not know?

DATE	VL	CD4	%	HDL
NOV 04	>1000000	31	2.85	4.3
JAN 05	2,038	115	5.0	6.4
FEB 05	165	159	7.8	5.9
MARCH 05	125	202	9.1	6.9
MAY 05	<50	168	10.0	7.0
JUNE 05	<50	199	11.8	7.2
JULY 05	<50	209	11.06	6.4
SEPT 05	56	205	11.9	6.1
NOV 05	<40	204	12%	6.4
FEB 06	<40	260	13.1%	6.7
MAY 06	<40	248	14.4%	6.4
AUG 06	<40	366	15.6%	6.0
NOV 06	<40	356	16.8%	6.2
FEB 07	80	244	17.1%	7.3

| MAY07 | <40 | 249 | 17.9% | 6.7 |
| AUG07 | <40 | 326 | 17.2% | 6.2 |

I became obsessed with my 'numbers' as they were known. In those days, as I was somewhat still at risk, I was tested every month and I rigorously kept a note in a chart of what they were, as if seeing it in writing made it real. Seems a bit sad now, but at the time it made the fact I probably WASN'T going to die more tangible.

I kept it up for three years, but it became somewhat redundant as clearly if I was still writing it, I was still around. Those months, years were very difficult and My Chart was a security blanket, proof of my existence. I pored over those numbers, went into meltdown if my CD dropped, or remained stationery, and examined them for proof that all was well.

What I WASN'T told about however, maybe because it was generally held to be A Good Thing, was 'Immune Reconstitution Syndrome' or IRS. Without going into the medicine and science of it (I can if you want – I became an expert....!) it basically means that when the drugs begin to work, your immune system rebuilds rapidly, as you can see by the numbers, and because of that, it starts to react and attacks things that have lain dormant in your system that it would normally have ignored. So. I got hairy leucoplakia, a severe oral thrush infection, and swollen lymph nodes (more of which later) and....yay!, Shingles. THE most painful thing I have ever experienced. The kind round your head and face and eyes...lovely. The trigeminal nerve that affects the face, jaw, gums, ears, scalp and eyes. The IRS had awoken the herpes virus we all have dormant in the base of our spines and BLAM. I could barely, speak, smile, laugh, lay my head down, wash, chew....anything, any SLIGHT movement which caused my skin to move was agonizing. Plus, I looked like a Klingon.

The result of this, apart from the GUM staff all nodding and going *"ooooh, them scabs are coming on nicely, eh?"* was drugs. Drugs by the bucketful. I had amitriptyline for the shingles, fluconazole for the thrush, antiviral medication for the leukoplakia, zopiclone to help me sleep through the pain, Tenofovir, Emtricitabine and Efavirenz for the HIV, prochlorperazin for the nausea (which I didn't actually have) and something else for the glands which were swollen, Terbinafine for a fungal infection in my toe, 17 in all, more than I can remember the names of. Everyday. Until the infections disappeared, one by one.

The bitter irony of this was not lost on me. I had taken Chris down to Newquay once during a school holiday, and I remember my Mum saying, in a hurried whispered conversation (in the very same bedroom my Dad had caught me sucking Peter off! Lol what irony!), *"He's a very nice boy, you know….for one of those. I hope you're being careful?"* (Mother, what ARE you implying??). *"There's this awful new disease going round. I saw it on the telly. They had lilies and everything. And that nice John Hurt."*

It was the absolute worst time of my life; I am so sorry now for the *schadenfreude* I felt when I was nursing clients at the respite house, for thinking *'Phew! That's lucky! THAT could've been me!!'* when actually, for 18 years…it was!

All this, for a fuck, long, long ago, probably drunken and probably shit anyway.

So, for the next few weeks it was sleep, take drugs, cry, drive on an endless conveyer belt of misery and fear. I had no plan about how to deal with it yet. Still no – one knew, and my whole universe revolved around the GU clinic and my bed, where I could sleep and escape, just for a while. The shock of this was profound and David really didn't know how to deal with it apart from being practical – feeding me, getting me to my appointments and trying to reassure me, mostly failing on that one. I kind of knew that, by now, I wasn't going to die, at least not in the short term. What was SO devastating, so utterly traumatizing was the fact of HAVING it, all these years, through all my travels and adventures, and not having a clue. I cannot describe adequately how this felt to me. The shock, the horror was SO deep, so overwhelming, I had no idea how to move forward. In addition to which, I was beginning to feel pain in my legs and feet, as the IRS continued along its jolly way. The nerves in my extremities had been damaged by 18 years of viral assault and now I had 'peripheral neuropathy' as well. Hurrah! Could it get worse? Well, yes actually – I'll tell you about that in a minute, you GHOULS!!

As my system was reawakened, more things became clear. The virus had threaded its stealthy way into my brain – I look back and realized how slow of thought, how forgetful, I had become. As the HAART worked, so my brain function improved. But so too did the knowledge that my hearing had become damaged; I began to be able to drive at night again so it seemed that it was in my eyes too, as my night vision had deteriorated so badly I couldn't see at night;

the pain in my reawakened nerves was getting worse. The only way to describe how it felt is as if boiling water had been poured on them, or bad sunburn. So, joy of joys – more drugs! Pregabablin. Does the trick – I'd have taken anything to stop it hurting. I take them now, still. If I miss one, the pain returns after about 18 hours, distant at first, then more and more insistent until it is unbearable. So, another legacy. Another Forever drug.

I noticed too that I had a small lump in the back of my throat. On telling Nicki, she sent me to ENT (another day, another department) whereupon the utterly GORGEOUS consultant said that he would like a biopsy done on the lump, *"just in case; probably nothing, but better to be safe, eh?"* and was scheduled for three days' time. Bloody hell - that was quick……

So, back to hospital again. Different department, same fear. Bearing in mind I was mid – shingles and I couldn't bear to be touched in any way, here I was, facing throat examinations…..I was put in a 'private' room (as in: 'HE'S GOT AIDS – KEEP HIM AWAY FROM US'. Actually, I HADN'T by this stage, so FUCK. YOU. Nice quiet room though) and told I'd be first in the morning. Obviously I didn't sleep as I couldn't put my head on the pillow and my amitriptyline wasn't due yet. I was NBM, and bloody starving.

Morning came and so did a consultant who said, actually, I was to be LAST, because they'd have to disinfect the theatre afterwards so last in the day was best, didn't I agree? I agreed, dumbly. I'm not sure if I understood the implications of what he meant until long after – too full of sorrow and self-pity to think very widely but clearly they'd decided the AIDS guy should go last. And that's what happened. After a 9 hour wait they came to get me, put me on the trolley and wheeled me down. Most undignified, those gowns, eh? Arse hanging out. Dimly aware if my arse *hadn't hung out* all those years ago, I wouldn't be here now… I asked what he was injecting me with and he told me it was penguin milk. Before I had chance to answer, I was gone and then woke up in recovery. Sore throat, job done.

I just needed to get the all clear and get on with trying to reassemble my former life, and get back to the time before my whole existence had been blown apart.

Then it got worse.

  It was cancer.

Oh yes, my dear friends. What wonderful news! Still reeling from my HIV diagnosis, still trying to believe my disgusting death was not imminent as I first thought, I get told I have the big C.

I got a letter (from my hunky ENT man) to say my result was with him at Bodmin hospital, nice and local. We could go and get it then nip down ASDA. That was the plan. We went into his office and there he was, all hairy and muscly (I know – some things you just can't help…!) on his swivel chair. He asked me to sit down and then he said: *"Wjf sdofm\cpsdmi\hsgh zdhfoz a4ut 4jsmofjmv\[ej sd\p \of **CANCER** moef\sopebnan040ubnt0weitv-]3tn idfzjbrjgp- &^$^^%&%(*Ylo"*

I just stared at him, with the Word bouncing madly off the walls, into my ears, out again, into my head……

Realising I hadn't heard, he repeated what he said:" *I'm afraid it's positive. You have Non – Hodgkinson's Lymphoma, but don't worry!! It's very early, and very treatable…."*

Oh, that's OK then. I must've been REAL bad in a former life to deserve this……AIDS, HIV and now CANCER! How fabulous. Again, it was one of those blank, buzzing kind of moments, where the world grinds into slow motion, just like they say on the telly. I heard nothing more but the hammering of my own heart, saw nothing but the swirly brown carpet as I felt all hope, so recently regained, drain from me into pools of despair. Still, I suppose if I was going to die, it would be from a respectable disease and they wouldn't have to lie on my headstone.

I think I said, *"Oh, ok."* But I don't really remember.

So, it began again – same crushing fear, just a different department at the hospital. 'Oncology'. Just a small blue door, innocuous, but holding behind it a mass of suffering; wasting, rotting humans who come with high hopes, some hope or no hope at all and varying amounts of hair and time in this world.

Amazingly, my consultant had got me a CAT scan for the next day; good and bad. Good because there was no waiting, no time to breed fear, and bad because if it was so 'treatable', what was the hurry?

The next day – it was a Thursday - I went to the scanner department and it was full. Full of defeated people with dull eyes, sitting, waiting for the big machine to tell them the worst. Somehow, I was taken right to the front, forced to drink a pint of vile milky stuff, which reacts and flags up any tumours or evil within. Slapped on the bed, strapped into place and slid silently into the maw of this thing, this thing that would tell them how long I had left to live. I was, I recall, weirdly calm, intrigued almost. It was quick and painless, not like the death that I was now certain was near would be.

That was that. Another week's wait and back to the blue door, back to confusion, fear, raging hatred against this new thing that was happening to me. Today was 'Bone Marrow Day', which consisted of lying on a bed while the specialist gave me an anaesthetic, for the pain that was to come, although he did say that once he was drilling into the bone, the pain killer wouldn't work but that bit wouldn't last long......I'd rather not have known, thank you. The nurse, who was just lovely, was very reassuring whilst he drilled into my hip bone, asking me about Hungary and teaching, but hey, actually, it really *didn't* work...the massive drill bit removing a piece of bone from my hip was rather more present than the conversation I was trying to have. JESUS BLOODY CHRIST – that was excruciatingly painful, and that was WITH the anaesthetic. *"All done"* he said cheerily, *"Here it is!"* holding up a glass slide with my bone marrow already squashed upon it. *"You may have a little bruising,"* he said. You could say that – it stretched from my behind my knee to half way up my ribs and my arse was completely blue and yellow.

I told my oncologist that I was experiencing sharp pains in the centre of my spine; probing and touching revealed nothing so he arranged an MRI scan for a couple of days' time (again.....bit worrying....) to check. Seven bloody thirty in the morning, though looking back, I realize how much they were doing for me. I suspect, because all the departments are interlinked, Nicki may have told them about me and how horrified and traumatized I had been over my HIV and so they were being especially accommodating and kind to me. Whatever the reason am really truly grateful to you all. It was a horrible horrible time for me and the care you took of me enabled me to cope – I felt I was really being looked after. Anyway the MRI scan went OK. One good thing – bizarre as it may sound – I heard, for the first time, Carly Simon singing (INSIDE the scanner!) *'Let the River Run'*. What a great song! Not the best place to discover it maybe, but one small victory over death!

Another week to wait. How people who are really in the throes of their disease cope with this staging, this waiting bit by bit, I don't know. Braver men than I am, Gunga Din. But, as always the time came round, and we were hospital bound once more. Another wait, seven days. Seven long days and nights full of fear and tears; terror and worst – case scenarios, but somehow they passed, and there we were in the car, heading back to the Blue Door, to see if the cancer had spread, to where and, as I was thinking, to find out how long I had left. I felt sick with fear, unable to walk properly, being held up like a crippled man.

My specialist sat me down and we began to discuss when we would begin the chemo. (not 'if', but when) and to say it was good news. The tests from the CAT and bone marrow were clear. No metastasis. Nothing from the MRI. No tumours there. Only NHL. Hahahhaaaa ONLY…… He said we should begin next week, with CHOPS, the gold standard of chemo drugs. I knew all about the side effects so that discussion was not to be had. But……I had spent the past few months rebuilding my fucked up, virus – ravaged immune system and I wanted to know what effect the drugs would have PLUS, as no-one was talking about this, whether there would be any contraindications with my ARVs. So I said, *"Will the immune suppression be severe?"* (or something. I'm not sure if I was able to construct a proper sentence, but my meaning was clear. Most of this is kind of pieced together from a memory that was severely compromised during this whole episode.). *"Only, since my diagnosis, I have discovered my immune system has been very weak, as it is."*

"What diagnosis?"

"my ..erm…HIV diagnosis…?"

"Oh. I see. I had no idea. Nobody informed me of this. This puts things in a different light altogether. I have never knowingly treated anyone with HIV with chemo drugs before. I have no idea what will happen."

Wow. That was so *comforting*! So – *what*? I can't have chemo because I have HIV so we'll just let the cancer kill me instead? This was getting better by the minute.

"Excuse me," he said and left the room.

He returned, looking harassed, angry, upset. *"I'm really sorry about this. I should have been told and wasn't and I have to confess to being somewhat under informed in this area. I have just contacted London College Hospital to ask them to look at your biopsy as it may have a bearing on what treatment we can give. I hope you understand that this is not my doing, but am doing all that I can to put it right and ensure the best outcome for you. I have expressed the tissue sample to them and I will contact you by phone when they have given me some advice."*

There wasn't much to say. We left. More waiting.

The days dragged by. We tried to be normal, go and see people, eat, watch telly but there was a massive black cloud, immovable, unforgettable.

Several people rang during those days. Each ring heralded disaster and I made David answer the phone each time. Finally, one afternoon, the phone went at it was him. I picked it up as I was standing right beside it and whispered, *"Hello?"*

"It's Treliske Oncology here. I have had the result back from UCL and…….."

My heart beating. My horizons narrowing. My life span in the balance.

"……..they say it is only a clump of cells, enlarged by one of your autoimmune responses. You actually don't have cancer."

"Hello? Hello, Mr Bray? ….Are you there?....Mr Bray…??

I had dropped the phone and it had slid under the desk from where the tinny voice of the consultant could be heard.

David picked it up and spoke to him. I have no idea what was said, what else I needed to know. All I knew was that I had cancer, and now, actually, I didn't. It was a mistake. An error. A booboo. Ooops! It was the weirdest thing – it was like I had planned a massive party and no-one had turned up. It was like a disappointment. I had absolutely NO IDEA how to react. I think I just wept.

No more fear? No more nights of tears and screaming in moonlit rooms, shouting

"GODYOU'REAFUCKINGBASTARDLEAVEMEALONEDON'T YOUTHINKI'VEHADENOUGH???????"

into the darkness, sobbing, consumed with self-pity and so aware of the irony…..

It wasn't until a few days had passed that the reality of the situation began to sink in. I had become so convinced, so married to the idea that I had **CANCER** and therefore was almost dead, that there was suddenly a massive hole where all the terror used to be. In an instant. They'd made a mistake, had filled me with chemicals, drilled a hole in my pelvis, irradiated me – and it was a *MISTAKE*? And you know what? All I could feel was gratitude. I should be "suing their fucking asses off" apparently, but all I felt was joy, release, love for the unknown doctor in London who had allowed me to live. Yay! I only had AIDS after all!

Actually, no I didn't, not any more. I had been declassified! Check *ME* out! All of the 'syndromes' that classified me as having AIDS were either being treated, going or gone. The bucket of drugs I had to take at first was gradually decreasing, there was word that those clever people at Gilead had managed to combine two of the antiretrovirals (ARVs hereafter – if you think I'm typing all that every time you've got another think coming, as my sainted Lady Mother used to say) into one pill, thereby reducing the load by another one…..I was feeling quite well, relatively speaking and couldn't wait to tell everyone my good news! YAY! I was going to live! I didn't have it, after all, so you can all stop crying and whispering when I come in to the room and patting me kindly…..

"You've got chemo on Tuesday, remember," David said. What? No I don't, I'm cured! Well, not *cured,* as I was never sick in the first place. *"What do you mean, I've got chemo?"*

"You've got chemo the third Tuesday of every month. It's in the diary."

"Whoa…..I DON'T NEED CHEMO. HELLO?"

"Yes you do. We've told everyone now, so we have to stick to it. No answering the phone for a couple of days after, because you'll be sick, but we can go out again by the following Saturday."

I was suddenly in a parallel dimension……I didn't understand…..why would you be doing this? I want to tell EVERYBODY!!! I don't want to have to sit and watch Lou, a Macmillan nurse, all too aware of the endings, quietly weep over dinner for her good friend who has the disease she witnesses every day; to see the terror and hope in my sister's eyes, to watch Mary and Jean be jolly and pretend it's OK when their hearts are breaking; to have my friends speak in that funny way around me – you know, the 'Cancer Voice'……why aren't we just TELLING THEM? Stop their sorrow, ease their pain? *"Because," he says, "it's in the diary. Chemo. Tuesday."*

Looking back, trying to analyse this, I have still come up with no better theory as to why he chose this option: either he needed to control the situation or was reluctant to be part of the celebration that would surely ensue. WHY that might be, I really cannot make sense of or find a valid reason for. It just was.

Or, maybe, it was that, you know, *CANCER* (whispered, Les Dawson face) is a far more presentable disease. Look! It's even got a Foundation! SO, maybe, by continuing the pretence of me having IT, and knowing I was recovering from my HIV illnesses, having chemo for a few weeks would coincide and voila! I'd be better and nobody would be any the wiser! Well, if that WAS it, it was cruel, both to all of the people crying for me and to me as I was weak and vulnerable and even more likely to agree, no matter HOW outlandish it was.

But, we did it. We're both to blame I guess.

But, looking back at this I am stunned by my passivity, my utter failure in being coerced; I just agreed. It was kind of OK because I KNEW that I would 'get better', that the chemo 'would work', but it was bitterly painful when people, joyfully, would say. *"You're handling the chemo well. Most people have a terrible time"*. *"Oh,* "I say, *"I'm just lucky with it"…*

Lies. Dreadful deceiving of the people I loved the most; as 'Chemo Tuesday' came round, it would be: "Ah, here I go again. It's awful, but don't worry everyone, it's working", inventing conversations I never had with my Oncologist, staying indoors for four days because I was too sick, too tired.

Lies. What was I thinking? They all deserved better, and yet, dear readers, to this day, that deceit has held firm. As far as they all know, I am a Cancer Survivor. Well done me. But, all I feel is shame. Shame. Shame for lying. Shame for allowing such a terrible thing to happen. And disgust at myself for being so led, so controlled, so pathetic. And that, dear reader, was, without a doubt, the thing that caused the breakup of our marriage, and caused my wandering to begin.

One of the strangest threads woven into this awful tapestry was a conversation I had with Anna, and with myself ever since. She was one of the first (and at that time, only) to know. I knew she would not judge. With Anna, everything had a reason and an outcome. As I sat sobbing in her chair, where I had sat so often, batting arguments, learning about the power of herbs, learning how to channel, to deal with ego, how the cerebrospinal fluid moved in waves, like a breath and how the healing crises happened in between its gentle rising and falling, all this back in the good old days before I had become a vile thing, a man of poison and grief....I was sitting there, hoping she would find something in her heart or from spirit to assuage the tsunami of grief that was constantly overwhelming and threatening to drown me, when she looked at me and said the most fucking stupid thing I had ever heard. Of course, she, as always, was right, and it took much work and much time to see this. After doing that narrow – eyed thing she does when she's listening intently, she said:

"I think you've got HIV as a learning tool. It's a kind of gift, I think".

I was rendered sobless. I stared at her, in disbelief. Anyone else, and I would have laughed and left. But it was Anna.

"What? WHAT? What do you mean???"

"I think for you to truly be at peace with yourself, to love yourself truly and completely, you need to be in a place where you are faced absolutely with the truth of being homosexual, and it seems that there is nothing more powerful than getting the one thing that characterises the fear and stigma and prejudice of that. Your day to day life had become complacent and you had stopped dealing with the troubling aspect of your relationship with your father. This is a spur to you, the most powerful symbol of all he loathes in you. You have been sent this as a weapon, a way of coming to terms with this. You will live and have good health, I say to you now, but this new struggle is positive outcome for you to truly live at peace with who you are......"

And she suddenly came back to the room and it became clear she had been channelling, I don't know who her guides are, but it was a very powerful message. Now, years later, I see it to be the truth, but then, in that room, at the darkest of all times, it was an utter pile of shite.

My life with HIV and its associated drug use continued, as of course it would have, still does, and will do for ever. The neuropathy increased, strangely always most painful from mid-evening onwards; feet rubbing helped, but it was always a reminder of it. IT. This thing, lurking in my guts, poisoning my heart, my social life, my every day. Nicki's words hadn't yet come true. Yes, I was better, far better, not nearly dead like before (Christ, you saw my passport photo…How could I not have known?) but I was still raging, full of hatred for the cunt who gave it to me (the logic of it having been a consensual shag didn't apply) and it coloured my every moment.

Forgive my indulgence here in a novel but I want to insert the poem I wrote, in the darkest of those times. Maybe it will show you, in a way that my prose cannot, the depths of my feelings at this time.

February 5 2005

Lines From A Dark Place.

Stare more into the dark.

Stare more into my dark

- and the sun does not rise, still.

I look at you from the corner of my eye,

Not daring to look at the thing you truly mean

And all I see is my death

      my despair

      my foulness

and I cannot unknit you form my heart, my DNA

and cannot too learn how to carry your poison.

I hate you for all the things you have robbed me of:

Fearlessness and compassion;

The skills to use my skills;

the beautiful Danube and of wonders undiscovered;

of the time before you ate into my

Tissues and atoms and heart, and man-ness.

You define me – I hate you

You fill me – I hate you

You complicate me – I hate you

You terrify me – I hate you

You steal me – I hate you

I hate you and I hate you.

    I cannot leave you.

    I cannot divorce you.

    I cannot bleed you.

    I cannot kill you away

    And I cannot live beside you.

I have no therapy

I have no hope of redemption

I have no respite from you; all my days ARE you.

I have blue fear.

I have ever more tomorrows of the things you cause.

I have little patience

I am left with songs I can no longer sing,

colours I can no longer paint,

the touch of skin and breath I can no longer feel,

the smells of a past I no longer have,

the rage I can no longer control,

The pain I cause where it is never deserved

And a black hole, and the singularity, into which I pour my losses,

And fear against the dying of the Light.

This, as I read it back, is all a bit studenty, but it was all I had, the only way to express my sorrow and my rage at what had happened to me. At this stage, we didn't know if David was positive too – it was very likely, as we had been having unprotected sex for over 16 years, with him ejaculating inside me. So, as well as dealing with my horror and shame, I was overwhelmed with the thought that he TOO was going to be sick, get AIDS, die and it would be MY FAULT.

Or…..actually – maybe he'd been fucking around and HE'D infected ME? Another massive weight to carry – my man had not only been unfaithful, but he'd also given me HIV. None of this was logical or important – who had given what to whom was irrelevant. I had it and that was that. But in those dark days, nothing was certain. I'd escaped death, it seemed, but was condemned to an eternal damnation – no escape, no recourse, no undoing…..

"Hi," he said. "I'm Bill. A friend of Vince". A trace memory; October 87….. Bill. At Chris's funeral…one OF VINCE'S FRIENDS. WHO ALL HAD AIDS!!! Oh you fool! You drunken fool! A hairy chest, a generous groin, a bucket of gin and a virus. Of course. The months of searching, trawling my memories for someone or something to blame it on suddenly crystallises here: THIS is the most likely. Does having an answer help? No, actually. It just adds 'STUPID' to the list of self-appellations.

Well played, Mr. Lucky. Well played.

Of course. Bill. He'd given me the reason to move home. And HIV. But, my fault as much as his. Mea Culpa. I have searched and searched over the years for a cause, a point of reference, a reason, and answer. But I didn't come to this until now, until the writing of this story. It makes no practical difference but there's some small comfort in knowing it was actually an amazing shag. Not worth the price, of course, but at least it was meaningful. So now we know. Probably.

So Chris, you bastard, who was most certainly there at that event, watching and grinning from above, probably having an angelic wank as we fucked…..why didn't you stop me? You'd have known. You were supposed to look AFTER me, you fucking fuck. You fucking…you were supposed to be my best…..

…but wait.

Maybe he knew. Like Anna knew. Maybe he knew I'd be OK (in the end) but needed to go through it on my long journey to self-acceptance, as hard and fucking horrible as it was. Maybe he, in the end, engineered that fuck, drew Bill and me onto the same trajectory in order to, finally, enable my true happiness? If so it was a hard hard lesson, but one, now that I am actually grateful for. I see my life as gift, each and every day, something that I was not aware of before. So, you old cunt. Even after death, you did right by me.

Is this true, or a load of old bollocks? You decide….for me, it provided comfort.

This, from the American author and activist, Bruce Ward, in his memoir, entitled *'15 Years'* and used here with his permission, encapsulates perfectly the sorrow and loss I felt at this time:

'I wanted to close my eyes and click my heels and be back in that time, a time before AIDS, a time before loss, before fatigue and daily pills and doctor's offices and rejection and more loss. I wanted to return to joy, to hope, to the innocence of romantic love, to possibility. I wanted to be touched. I wanted my circle of friends to magically re-appear, like in the movie 'Longtime Companion'*, where all the dead gay men come back to dance on the beach at Fire Island. I want this alien ripped from my body…..*

…..For over a decade, my primary focus had been to stay alive…one day, one breath at a time. That had been my job. Everything else – career, love, finances, family, friends – became secondary. I had to learn how to live with the stigma of AIDS, on another planet, in another century, speaking a foreign language, in what Virginia Woolfe described as the 'undiscovered country' of illness….'

Fortunately, Bruce, we were both granted clemency and we made it, smaller, lonelier, but alive.

Gradually, gradually though, things became easier. I was very lucky with my medication – I didn't shit myself to death like some poor souls did; I didn't turn into the elephant man or the bloke from 'Scream'…..the gods were kind. Maybe making up for what they'd done to me eh?

But. But I STILL could not live with the deceit about the *facts*. All my friends and loved ones continued to watch anxiously to see if my cancer would recur – *'Lucky it was only Hodgkinson's Lymphoma, eh?'*, they'd say. Not anything serious like pancreas or prostate. I knew they still were scared, there were subtle changes in the way they spoke to me – kind of hushed, or by overcompensating and telling really shit jokes, the kind usually reserved for kids or old Aunts. Poor them. How I ached to say, to *scream*: "I DON'T HAVE 'AUTO-IMMUNE DISEASE, YOU KNOW 'LIKE THE ONE BARBRA WINDSOR HAD'. I DON'T HAVE CANCER! IT WAS LIES! ALL LIES!! I NEVER DID. I HAD AIDS. I HAVE HIV. I HAVE H.I. FUCKING V!" But I didn't. I remained mute. Silenced by embarrassment, fear, humiliation and him. You, reading this, probably have no idea what it is like to have a DISEASE (which is how I couldn't help thinking of it, still in capitals) which was universally feared, despised, judged and caused all kinds of religious, moral panic; which would cause people – yes even your friends and family – to be repulsed, to stop touching you. Of course this was only my perception of how it would be. I was probably doing these people a disservice; they would probably be understanding and grown up about it, educated and well versed in the facts. It was all a reflection of how I viewed MYSELF during this time: mendacious, full of shame and disease. It was becoming clear that more and more people were being infected; some celebrities – Andy Bell from Erasure, Holly Johnson from Frankie Goes to Hollywood – were 'disclosing' presumably to say: "Hey, it's OK. It's not your fault", and to spread sexual health awareness. But I couldn't. Just couldn't. I lived in fear and shame with my mouth full of stones.

We were in 2005 now and still my shoe size was the least important thing.

Suddenly I found myself living in a cloaked world, a world of secrets and lies. I was recovering, that was true, and my friends were pleased (if a little surprised at the smooth ride had, given all those 'Chemo Tuesdays' and the havoc they must have wrought) that I was getting better and being out in the world again. But the scales were SO unevenly weighted and with each well – wish, their side rose and mine sank, weighted down with my deception, guilt, self-loathing and degradation. I knew, I just knew, at some point in the not too distant future, I would be discovered and my disease riddled secret would be laid bare for all to see and pour their hatred upon. Of course, my rational head knew this would not be so, but I wasn't very big on 'rational' at that precise time. David was monitoring my every move, every word – though what he could have done had I made an announcement, I don't know, but still, he was on Damage Limitation Duty 24/7, particularly when I 'went next door' where inevitably I would get hammered and maybe loose lipped. *In vino veritas,* but not in this case – no one would ever know. Ever. (Except you, gentle readers, who now do!).

So, what did I do? I wrote to my best friends – Marion and Betty. BAM. Just like that. I was suddenly sure that if I didn't release this valve, my heart would burst for sorrow. So I wrote to them and then hid under my bed waiting for a reply, which when it came was so overwhelming and beautiful, so full of love and concern and of practical help on how I could stop being a twat and never to doubt our friendship again. Armed with the hope that it *would* maybe OK, I resolved to tell, actually SPEAK the words to my other friends, the ones near. David was absolutely against my doing this – I told him to fuck off. My life, my virus, my choice and maybe if you don't like it, then maybe you shouldn't have lied to them all. I wasn't though in the business of revenge – all I wanted was to have to stop lying.

I rang Louise, the Cancer nurse, and asked to see her, to which she agreed so I drove over and we sat in her lounge, both trembling, but robbed of speech. Eventually, I said:

"Lou, I have something to tell you…."

"……" no reply. Wide eyes, lip trembling.

"Ah! No, it's ok, the cancer hasn't come back… (you lying cunt! Now. EVEN NOW…….) *it's not that…"*

Looking less terrified, she said, *"OK, …what then…?"*

I couldn't move the stones in my mouth, they blocked the words…

"I……I have….I'm HIV+"

Silence. As I feared. Bracing myself for the rejection, I sat, downcast, waiting.

Eventually she said:

"Thank goodness…..I thought you were having an affair……."

Now, I don't know about you, dear reader, but those two things, in my view, don't carry *quite* the same weight, or stigma, or repulsion factor and the possibility of death, and so her reaction was a bit….unexpected but I came to see that she was less worried about me, as in this case, being in the medical profession, she was educated, knew the state of play with drugs, therapy, survival, prognoses, so actually, when I'd stopped feeling hurt by her apparently cavalier statement, I realised that she was in fact being positive and that I didn't bring news that was going to be awful for me, which (having just had a catastrophic affair herself) she perceived to be a Bad Thing. Big hugs, tears of relief, large gin and tonic, wobbly drive home (yes, I know – don't judge me, I was hardly 'rational' as I said) and the scales had moved back towards the centre, now just weighed down by the biggest lie of all to the two closest friends of all.

My friend came to stay, down from Oop North. We went out for the day, to Polperro, to Looe, to Talland Bay, to Fowey, it was beautiful, it was normal. We took the ferry to Polruan, had a beer, went up the hill to Battery Park and looked out over the sea. How could this be so normal? Nothing, NOTHING would ever be 'normal' again. Not with this this…thing inside me. We found a bench. We sat apart.

"Mads, I wanted to get out today. I have something to tell you" Why? Why did she need to know? I rarely saw her in reality – why fuck up her life? But it was like, now I couldn't help it. I wanted to say. The Words.

"Oh OK……….."What?"

"I……I……"

She looked expectantly…

"…have HIV".

….Just the crashing of the green waves on the rocks below, which five seconds earlier had been beautiful but was now a call to doom, and the gulls all crying: AIDS! AIDS!.....

"Oh. OK. Thanks for telling me." We hugged. Actually hugged, people! We went home. I told David what I'd done. He was furious – I guess he was unsure exactly how much I'd said, but I assured him I'd said no more than that – and, up till now, I haven't

Gill, and I respected her hugely for this, had gone off to America, to Boston. I mean PROPER gone, all her stuff and dog, spotted hankie over her shoulder, to seek a new life. She'd gone to live with Michael (my brother) initially and from then to get a better life in the Land of Plenty. It was so hard seeing her go, my ally, my playmate…

Gill's Last Day in Newquay, where we'd spent the day together.

   She did good – got some decorating work, made some really good friends and ended up driving a tractor on a tobacco plantation. Go girl! So when all this shit hit my fan, she was 3090 miles away and I could chat on the phone and she'd never know. But then I heard, as usual, the family dynamic fucked up and that she'd be coming back and was bound to see people so it was really important that it was ME that lied to her first. We met in a pub in Penryn and after some bravery water, I said,

"Squiggs, while you were away, I was diagnosed with cancer but I had chemo and check-ups and it's gone so I'm alright. Hey! Don't look so terrified! Really I'm fine now," all tumbled out in furious rush. *"My round. More beer?"*

OH! OH! OH! PANTS ON FIRE. Why, *WHY*, did I say cancer and not HIV? Because I was a fucking coward, and was ashamed and scared she'd reject me. That's why. And for that ALONE, I owe her a massive apology. She deserved better, she deserved the truth, but I was in too deep, caught in the web and so I toed the party line. She'd be told, by *somebody* I had cancer so I wanted her to know, from me, I wanted to lie to her *first* so I was able to reassure her that I was OK, that the cancer was gone. Oh! my shame is unbearable; her, of all people.

But I wanted too, to protect her from the truth, because I WAS better and she didn't *have* to know. But I said, in this story, I would tell the truth, the whole truth and nothing but – so, now she *CAN* know, and this very act has been more healing and empowering than you, dear readers, will ever know.

Coming Out. <u>COMING. OUT</u>. In capitals it looks more important. Because it is. The years of jigsaw puzzle making, as documented here by Mr. Lucky himself; the agonies of knowing you were different and that probably meant loneliness / rejection / beatings -up (delete as appropriate); the first time you step through your own Salisbury's Doors into Never Going Back land; the first time you tell someone, *anyone*, but in a whisper so you can pretend you only coughed if the look on the their face wasn't the right one; the opening of your big gay mouth but the words getting stuck behind your teeth every time so you just say *'Oh, nothing, doesn't matter'*; the standing by the pole, against the wall, blindfolded and handcuffed waiting for the firing squad hired by your parents, waiting for the gunshot that would kill your future and their love for you....all of this, as I look back and compare, WAS a piece of piss, compared to this, *this* COMING OUT, the gayest of all gay signs, attributes, stigmas, targets, *'serves you fucking right, you dirty queer'*s, scars, brands...*that* coming out was nothing. And Anna, Chris you were so right - if I could do *this*, I could do anything. But it has taken years, years, dear reader, and here I am, coming out again. To you. From the safety of these pages.

So. The Big One. You, reading this, probably have no idea of the terror I felt as I got in the car later that evening, a bit pissed for courage, a bit pissed so I could avoid being harassed by David to such an extent I'd bottle it. Down the road I'd driven so often, when I was normal, before I became a leper, a thing of disease and fear. Down to the house I'd been so many times, to all those dinners, all those parties, all those times of innocence and joy, to where I would utter words that would never be able to be unsaid and ones that I knew not how they would be heard.

David (no surprise there) had rung to tell them I was coming so they were expectant, fearful but sat side by side on the grey swirly settee, in solidarity as if by their proximity, they could ward off any danger or evil.

I sat. I looked. I said yes I would like a drink. Large please. We looked.

All the pebbles in my mouth tumbled to the floor and I said: *"I don't have an autoimmune disease, like Barbara Windsor* (oh, to have used Babs as a shield was reprehensible) *I have HIV."*

"We know", said Mary. *"We thought so all along. But we had to wait for you…"*

"It's OK with us", said Jean. *"Want another gin? And a fag?"*

"Yes, and yes", I gasped.

I just sobbed and sobbed and sobbed. We were done. And we never spoke of it again.

Actually, nobody did.

Which is a bit weird.

CHAPTER NINE.

INTO THE MADHOUSE.

In which our hero learns new skills, spends some time in Willy World and gets a present from that nice Tony Blair.

'Monster'.

by The Automatic. No.4. June 2006.

Bending, twisting, trying to find my way through….

~ ~ ~

Not much changed over the months. It was like nothing had happened. Everyone's life just carried on, as did mine, though I had a Big Secret from most people. Now though, I was in recovery (from Cancer! Lol) so my not being very well was just passed off as 'to be expected'. But it also meant I couldn't work. I really couldn't. My 'gift' was at this point not particularly useful. I had no money and nothing to do. Apart from being online, looking at porn mostly (when David wasn't around) which was ok except that it just made me depressed…Look! Look at those healthy men! Look at their big stiffies! Look at them shagging! Watch them come! It was now everything I was not. I hadn't had sex since before November last year, 11 / 11 / 11, for all sorts of complicated reasons…I felt ugly and diseased and not particularly shaggable. Also my libido had shrunk along with my dick – I just had no interest; it felt all wrong and David desperately wanking me off and insisting I come, when I had virtually no hard on, hurt and didn't really help, and it was really embarrassing. A self-fulfilling prophecy…the machinery of erections is so finely balanced it doesn't take much to cause it malfunction. Great. Fucking ED along with everything else. Back to the clinic. Appointment to see the willy man. Stupid questionnaires about doing sex….homework on how it feels. HORRIBLE, that's how, you idiot, but of course the more present The Problem became the worse it got. We were instructed to have sex, every day and write down what happened and how it felt. Really?

'Nothing' and *'Like shit'* were the answers. How likely was it, Robin, that I was going to want to have sex every day?

"No, it'll be good for the problem."

"I don't have a problem. I'm always rock hard, I am," said David. Not the most helpful interjection, actually.

"No, well, that's good. But its Nigel's problem we have to sort out, eh? Sex every day and keep a diary. That's the ticket."

Well, I did try. And failed. Oh, we did it, him saying, *"You'll never get better if we do don't what he says,"* and of course getting a daily shag, and me really wanting to be anywhere else but there, with his hands on my unwilling cock, trying to make me come. Then writing it down:

'Got erection. 1 minute. Lost it. Didn't come'

'Got erection but not hard.'

'Nothing happened. Kept trying as instructed. Failed'.

It was sad, it was excruciatingly embarrassing and served only to reinforce my loathing of the thing that I believed was cause it all – the foulness inside.

I don't know how it came about but the next thing I know, we're BOTH looking at porn. Tentatively at first, pretending we weren't really that interested, then joining Gaydar ("you know, just to see") and this quickly escalated into having threesomes! HOW? I have no idea, other than I suppose David might have wanted some proper sex, with someone who could get a hard on and come properly, you know, like a Real Man. We found ourselves online all the time and men were coming to the house with increasing frequency. Usually married men, on the way home from 'working late'- builders, high court judges, policemen, teachers, all passing through, all desperate for some anonymous sex, in an anonymous house on an anonymous estate, where it meant nothing after the final panting spurts. And how do you think it went for me, readers? Two virile men, two hard cocks, two loads shot, while I, impotent, infected with HIV, pretending to enjoy it, putting up barriers so that it was safe, safe, always safe, making excuses for my performance, being passed over for the man with the erection. It didn't feel that great, to be honest. But I didn't stop it. I didn't say no. I didn't make an excuse and leave. No matter how awful, there was still a cock to suck, someone to wank off.....and it was this imperative, dear reader, that had brought me to this place of disease and despair in the first place and yet still, the imperative to feel validated by having sex with a man overrode all else. Even then. I cannot explain this.

While all this was going on, I had made a decision to retrain as a...a..I didn't know, but a *something*, something to give my life some purpose, something to do, apart from having sex with strangers, in my bed. I found there was a free Computer Training Course in town and I thought website design might be interesting, if not ever useful. So I enrolled and went every day. New faces, new activity, new neurons woken. It was a piece of piss actually, but I did the whole course to make it last, finally getting a distinction, a City and Guilds in website design, and a lovely certificate to go in the folder next to my NPQH certificate (the only interesting part of which was, on a weekend away in The Grand Hotel in Torquay, getting pissed in the pub after the day's seminars and having the most amazing sex with a married man (you see? It never stops.) in his room. PROPER amazing, so that the next day, we snuck off and did it again instead of completing the 'Ancillary Staff Training' module), which I have never had any use for or recouped the hundreds of pounds it cost to send me on it.)

It was now Summer, 2006; I was still alive, at least. Against the odds.

- So here's the thing:
- I was HIV positive.
- I'd been *THIS* close from starting chemo for cancer I didn't have, which would have destroyed my immune system. Again.
- I am living a lie to everyone I know and love.
- I am living with a man who controls everything I do, and everyone I see.
- My life is controlled, micro managed, even to only being allowed 1 glass of wine, at 9.00pm, just 1 bowl of crisps from the bag of Kettle Chips.
- I am getting very drunk, a lot, as I am very unhappy.
- I am unemployed and we have no money.
- I am having sex with random strangers, having 3somes, being spit roasted, (safe, safe safe) even while knowing I am diseased.

- I can't get it up.
- I am full of self-loathing.
- I have constant peripheral neuropathy.

Things are really not great right now, and nobody knows, and I can't get it hugged away.

What to do? What to do?

So. I had a brainwave I know! I know how to fix this mess!

So, having made *sure* that this was a brilliant idea, a few night later, after our latest shag had gone (it might have been the one who wanted hot wax poured on his bollocks. I remember that one because he was a high court judge (I kid you not, dear reader), he had ginger pubes and no hard on and because it was the very worst....), I rolled over in bed, and said:

"David. Will you marry me?"

"Yes", he said. *"I've been waiting for you to ask. Yes I will. But it's not a marriage of course, it's a Civil Partnership."*

I fucking well *KNOW* that. That's not the point. Thanks for ruining the moment.

In 1453, someone left the gate open and the Turks got in and sacked Constantinople.

In 1788, the Austrian army attacked itself by accident, and lost 10,000 men.

In 1812, Napoleon decided to invade Russia. In Winter.

In 1937, the Hindenburg was launched. Filled with helium.

In 1962, Decca records turned down the Beatles, saying 'Guitar groups are on their way out'.

In 2006, I asked David to marry me.

This is up there with the Worst Decisions of All Time. I *DO* want to say that I blame him for nothing. He was what he was and in fact, I blame ME because I let it all happen. He was a controller, and I was the controllee. I was totally complicit in this dysfunctional relationship that everyone thought was so perfect and admirable. I am not setting out to diss him – I allowed it all, and so really, it's not his fault, it was mine, but it took years for me to realise it. Years to undo.

My motivation? Fuck knows. Let's see.....

Mr Lucky's Motivations:

- Maybe I thought marrying him *("It's not a marriage blah blah")* would make us 'equal'. Really?
- Maybe I thought it would mend all the things that were wrong in my heart and had been fermenting since leaving Hungary.
- Maybe I thought if I had a proper husband he'd be less likely to leave me for one of the men who came to the house for sex who had a dick that worked.
- Maybe I thought being married would make our relationship – TWO HOMOS! – valid in the eyes of the world.

- Maybe I thought it would make me *normal*. Like *you*.

Ah……getting to the crux. Acceptance. Especially NOW, although that was still my secret to keep. Would I ever disclose? Would I ever be able to say: *'Look here. HIV, in spite of its capital letters, is just a bug. A bug that is no danger to you, or to me actually, if I take my pills, which I do. It's no biggie'*. I doubt it. Though I was beginning to reach some kind of peace with myself, given that I was getting healthier and healthier, and that because I LOOKED well, nobody had to know (Let's forget the cancer-that-never-was. I'm a 'survivor' and it was, shamefully, a kind of cover story. Forgive me. I was weak. I should've spoken out but I didn't), I didn't expect for it to be common knowledge. Ever. My problems (long resolved) about being gay and the hatred and loathing of my Father would be finally crushed by this act of getting married. I'd be the same as you. See? Normal.

It was, dear reader, the biggest Elastoplast you've ever seen.

I ignored, completely ignored, all the feelings of disquiet as I got swept up in the preparations. Maybe it'd be OK. People were invited. Registered the intention, had Banns read, decided on outfits (Cornish tartan, thankyou), chose the venue, (our house) chose the date…

June 21st 2006. The Longest Day…

June 21st. Summer Solstice. The Longest Day. And I have to say, it was a wonderful one. I was very proud to be wearing the colours. We got up at dawn and watched the sunrise from the Beacon, had the service, cried like a girl, went on the Puffer Train as special surprise, went home, tried to have sex (married now, you know) and David fell asleep with my soft cock in his mouth. (About which I didn't feel too good). Got ready, went out to restaurant, ate till I felt sick. Went home. Stayed up till the Longest Day's end. Went to bed. My thanks to the two dear friends who made the day so memorable. Following week, massive party at home, EVERYONE invited, wedding cake with two grooms (one in tartan kilt. Awwww), food enough to feed an army, got drunk (no change there then) stayed up till the day's end again, went to bed. Started married life.

Which was exactly the same as unmarried life, only more trapped. Bollocks.

To quote my Canadian muse (on whom I had been calling often, just lately):

'After the rush when you come back down
You're always disappointed
Nothing seems to keep you high
Drive your bargains
Push your papers
Win your medals
Fuck your strangers
Don't it leave you on the empty side.'

(Joni Mitchell, 'Woman of Heart and Mind')

It was true. After all the excitement, it was business as usual – same old, same old. Trying to get business on the website front, 'fucking our strangers', and it was, indeed, leaving me on the empty side. I KNEW as I had uttered those four words, I was being a twat – how would this ever fix anything? I was getting bits of work, but depressingly few. It was a dying business really: either people already had a site, built it themselves, or got a mate to do it. For free, so why would they pay me? But still, it gave me a chance to be online, away from real life. When I wasn't, I was next door with a couple of bottles of wine, 'misbehaving' and being disapproved of - *"If you don't stop drinking you'll look like Jabba the Hut"*. Thanks for that. My self-image is shit enough as it is....

We were lost souls, Gaynor and I; her troubled past and my troubled future came together most synergistically into a troubled present, which we sought to resolve by blotting it out. Loud music, rollies and red wine – the holy trinity of escapism. David began to get regular house sitting requests and when he was away, the mice did most certainly play, and it wasn't pretty. We got so drunk, we were rendered incapable of speech sometimes, and unable to stand up, but always at hers. Her garden was a fairyland of lights and plants and nooks, quite the opposite of the clinical and anally retentive space next door. It was lovely to be outside there, with the candles in the trees, lit every single evening for the souls of all her animals, the chimenee blazing, the music floating and the wine smoothing out all the edges. It was Narnia, it was Secret Squirrel, it was delicious, I could sa *'Hullo clouds!, Hullo sky'* and skip abut like a gurl',and it was always too short a time. We had no secrets, she and I – all was laid bare, *in vino veritas* was the order of the day, all things spoken of...all, all but one, one that I dared not speak. You fool! You think she would've loved you any less? Judged you? Blamed you? No, stupid boy, she would have given you one of her bone crushing hugs and a kiss, given you a slap for not trusting her enough and then opened another bottle. I am sorry – I should've treated you better. I hope you can understand why? I might've even have found the courage to have told you, but I had been forbidden, by my Master, who didn't want you *"blabbing it all over the place when she's pissed"*. Maybe you would've, who knows, but its ME who had it, not him.....or maybe *that* was the problem and he didn't want to be guilty by association. That's why I was forbidden to speak of it, and why he was so angry when I told those dear few, the ones I wanted to know that I wasn't dying and to stop their hearts breaking. So, dear friend, my silence was required and once more, I acquiesced without a murmur.

We partied the nights away, she and I; Running, running. We lost whole weekends, but nothing got any better, nothing changed. Her past continued to haunt her and my future continued to be uncertain. But we loved each other deeply; we were connected in ways that nobody else understood. She was loud, brash, rude, often drunk, lairy, but I knew the woman beneath all the bluster, and we held each other up. That old bollocks about crossing paths with the people you were meant to certainly applied here, and was not, in this instance 'old bollocks'. She loved wood, the sea, the hawks and the buzzards, jasmine, beads, Mary Chapin Carpenter and me. And I betrayed her, dear reader, due to being such a weak man; lied to her over and over because I was instructed to.

Utterly pathetic. But, for now, we sailed on, having no idea of the tempest that lay ahead.

Unhappy me, internet, time alone...the Perfect Storm.

Typing, alone at night. Just a single lonely light shining on my keyboard. Looking at hairy men on BearWWW. No chance of having a wank, obvs, as much as I'd like to have done.

Click. Click. Click....Oooh, HE'S nice....

The first picture of Si I ever saw. Scrubs up nice, eh?

'Hi'.

Tick.. tick.. no reply. Then, ping!

'Hi'. (Two 'Hi's...what could this mean? Nothing, you twat. He wasn't real.)

'Why are you called 'Shoemaker'?'

'Because I make shoes'.

'Oh. LOL'

'I see you make websites.'

''Yep.'

I was here to see if he had a big cock, a hairy chest, what he liked, not to talk about websites.....I was just about to log out and go searching for the next usually faceless profile of a man I would never meet, when he replied:

'Oh that's good then. I need one. For my business. Would you be interested?'

'Um, yes I suppose so.....'

There are thousands of men on line, searching gay chat sites, that night and every night; hundreds of sites, dozens of time zones, tens of thousands of profiles. What are the chances of this bloke stumbling across mine, not wanting to see my cock (just as well) but needing a website? Infinitesimally small, I'd say. Or just Lucky....

'Your profile says you do reiki too? Is that why you're 'Reikiman?'

Like DUH...*'Yes,'*

'So do I.'

'I'm a bit tired actually. Nice to chat to you. Bye'. And I logged out.

How strange – someone who didn't say 'put your cam on, I'm horny and want a wank with you'. Too drunk to stay up, I went to my large bed, with only me in it.

> *'Woke up this morning feelin' fine*
>
> *There's something special on my mind*
>
> *Last night I met a new girl in the neighbourhood, whoa yeah*
>
> *Something tells me I'm into something good....'*

Like Herman, strangely I had something special on my mind. I'd spent so many empty nights online, post wine - quaffing next door, and it was always the same and given my ...ahem...temporary condition, mostly fruitless. Yet last night, I'd met someone who'd actually asked about ME, not how big my dick was or whether I take it up the ass. Like, as a *person*. And that was really cool. Trouble was, being as drunk as I was, I wasn't sure I would be able to find him again, amongst the oceans of flotsam on the gay sites. Or is jetsam? Whatever – I wasn't even sure what site it was now. Gaydar? Silver Daddies – could be; that's where I met the man who came to stay, had sex with us, took us out to dinner and, later saved me…..he has become a long standing a dear friend, in spite of finding himself in a not especially pleasant sexual scenario which, dear readers, I will spare you from. DudesNude? No……ah well. Never mind. I'm a married man (*"Civilly Partnered"*. Shut *UP*) so it's irrelevant. It was yet another empty internet night.

'*You've got mail!"* said Joanna Lumley in her cheery Roedean voice. And there was a message for me, from BearWWW. That's it! Forgot that one. Only ONE bottle of wine tonight, missis! It was still play weekend. I'm allowed….

'Hello. How's you? Nice to talk to you last night. Lovely smile. Don't forget my website. Simon.'

Ohmygodohmygodohmygod….what? What was happening? Be still my beating heart! I think I was so unused to anybody saying anything nice that this seemed very special. *'SIMON!'* So I logged on.

He wasn't there.

'Hi Shoemaker Simon. Got your message. No, I hadn't forgotten (Pants on fire) *so let's talk about it.'*

David came home on Sunday.

"*What have you been up to then? Anything nice*?" though he knew I would've spent most of it next door, with *'that woman'* (to whom he was more than friendly and pleasant to her face).

"*Not much. Oooh, I think I've got a new job though. Website thing. Someone online contacted me.*"

"*Oh that's good. We could do with the money*". Not 'Congratulations' or 'Well done'. "*Who is it?*"

"*Someone called Simon. From London.*"

"*Gay?*"

I'd have to tell him where from I suppose though as he's been picking up trade on Gaydar for months, I think the moral high ground isn't something he could take here.

"Yes. BearWWW. It's a site for….erm….bears."

"Oh."

"Early days yet." I said, moving swiftly on. "We've got a meeting to talk about it. He's got a business and a house in France or something and he needs all the bits tying together."

"When's the meeting? It'll be interesting to see him." Yeah, got the subtext.

"I don't know. I just have to see when he's on line and we can put our cams on and chat then."

This happened fairly quickly (though not soon enough for me) and there he was….better looking than in his profile picture, and the same age as quoted, not in Gay years (which is unusual, believe me.)

I don't remember the chat very well; it was very business-like, things to sort, and being monitored didn't help. It seemed like he was an advocate and activist for gay rights, and disabled people, a theatre designer, a researcher and he also owned a tumble down house in France. He wanted it put together in one place, and I, still not very experienced, found it quite a challenge. This required me to be constantly asking questions about the how and the where of things, and when David wasn't around, more personal stuff – he'd worked for the Royal Ballet, he'd met Nuryev, Elaine Paige, knew Fenella Fielding…..I was, I have to admit, a bit star struck, and I was being drawn deeper and deeper into his world, a world that spoke to my heart as was he into mine, such as it was….he was the nicest, most gentle, funniest, kindest man I think I had ever met. Well, when I say 'met'…..you know what I mean. He was *'single, 47, moderately hairy and'*…..I'm not telling you the rest, actually. But he sounded wonderful.

Eventually, over time, we began to 'need' to speak on the phone – the messaging 'wasn't immediate enough', and I could then hear his voice. It was soft and utterly engaging, he was funny and inquisitive, respectful of my situation and also professional – he was, after all, paying me for this. By now, I would have done it for free, just to be able to ring him, at what was becoming daily intervals. Still, the website was coming together and everything seemed to be above board and I realised that if it was finished, then so would this…this…thing that was clearly developing far beyond what was actually being said…..

Hardly daring to believe what I was about to do, I said to David, *"This website is proving to be a real sod to finish so we, Simon and I, thought that if he came down to visit with his laptop, where I could actually see what he meant – it's really difficult, even on the phone –we could sit together and get it done. Then I'd get paid. You like him don't you?"*

"Hmm not a bad idea. It's been going for ages. Probably time to wrap it up now. OK, yes."

What *his* true motives were, I never discovered. Another shag? Checking out possible competition? Or neither. Maybe it was just a good idea.

So, I suggested it to Simon, and we arranged a date. Wednesday April 4th. 18.15 Bodmin Parkway.

And there **I met the man who was to mend my heart and break David's.**

CHAPTER TEN.

JERICHO.

In which everything tumbles down like a tumbling thing at the World Tumbling Championships, I Come Out (again) and plan The Great Escape (sort of).

'Breathe Easy'

by Blue. No.6. April 4th 2007.

There's no air! I couldn't breathe, or sleep now, without you next to me.

~ ~ ~

After a kerfuffle about not being able to come because he had no money *("No its fine! It's fine! I'll pay for everything!!"* Down boy, you're like a bitch on heat), Simon boarded the 14.06 from Paddington and set off on what would turn out to be strangest, amazingest, fabulousest journey of his life. 'Cos that's the day he meets Mr. Lucky!

As he speeds towards Bodmin, I am preparing a 47 course dinner; well, OK, 3, but it's well special. I have shaved, showered and, as Bette Midler once said: *'FDS'd myself into a stupor'*, only with cologne. I smell like a whore's handbag. *'Miss Dior? More like 'Foggy Trollope'* as dear Rodney would've said. David is bemused, wondering why I am fannying about like a mad thing, assuming that I'm just looking forward to a shag (which we'd discussed, agreed and planned –

anything to get into Simon's pants) whereas I in fact, am already giddy with dread and excitement and, well, OK, lust.

We drove to the station, me in a panic, a giddy whirl – I had no idea what to expect from this meeting only that it was imperative that it had to happen. Maybe it would be a business meeting and I'd finish the website, he'd pay me and he'd go home; maybe it would be a couple of shags (as we 'always play together', he'd better be up for a 3 – way); maybe it would just be a nice weekend, meeting a new friend. Or all three. Option four was shoved firmly to the back of my mind.

I had already, to backtrack a little – I don't want you to think I'm just anybody's you know – gone up to Devon as Head Teacher on Summer School teaching French exchange students and there I met Bruce, with whom I immediately fell, like totes in love, and wanted to live with. He was only recently (bitterly) divorced and out, - Boy, was he OUT! - and he was making up for lost time, astonished that all the subterfuge of shagging behind his wife's back (see?) could stop and he was clearly aiming to win the Mr. Randy trophy in this year's Mr. Randy Competition. I'd leave work, head into town, meet him in the pub and we'd go back to his and have so much sex you wouldn't think we could fit it in (actually, we couldn't but that's another story) before having to get up and go back to work. Bonk, bonk, bonk. I was bleddy knackered. He was a sweetheart, but wouldn't marry me 'cos he had way too much shagging to do and with everyone in sight. I drove away, tear stained and desperate, David Gray's *'Alibi'* shaking the windows of the car.

You have to wonder where my head was at....I had a husband *(CIVIL PARTNER!!!)* at home, a mortgage, a new job with a language school, a house – how could I POSSIBLY live with Bruce? I barely knew him – very nice, great (extremely safe) sex etc, but really?.....Was I *SO* desperate to avoid having to go back to *there*...? I even stopped at Anne's Burger Wagon, in a layby on Bodmin Moor and texted him, begging him to change his mind but one of his clients had just shit himself in Tesco so he was a bit busy...I've heard of some excuses, but really...

Another time, and bizarrely with little protest, I announced I needed to get away for a few days and went to spend the weekend in Windsor with the man who had stayed at ours a few weeks earlier. He'd said, when we parted in

ASDA's carpark, *"Look, if you ever need to get away…."*. Wise man. What had he seen? Stuff I was refusing to? *"You're always welcome at mine…"* After a heart-breaking hug he drove away, but a few weeks later, I rang him and went to stay. Same pattern as before. Fell in love, had loads of excellent (and very safe) sex – with an *erection*, thank you very much; a minor detail for you, but a major one for me. I don't think any further explanation is necessary – and then asked, like a twat, if I could move in.

"Erm…no," he said.

"WAAAAAAH! AWWWWWWWW!! WHY NOT?" I wailed.

Same reasons, as above. Went home, kept texting the poor man, like a stupid child, on the train, but (thank goodness) he held firm. Not that he didn't like me; he did (he does) but could see a whole shit storm heading his way which he wanted no part of. Right choice. Right choice.

So you see, I had already made two (totally unrealistic and unsuccessful) bids for freedom, and now this Simon was heading my way…..what could it mean? My insides were like jelly, it was like being in love again, right at the start, when you're a bit breathless and you do a small wee. AND I didn't even know the bloke, though it felt like I always had.

'The train arriving on platform 2, is the 14.06 from Paddington.' I (apparently) was running up and down the platform like a fucking eejit, going *"Where is he? Where is he? I can't see him! Where is he?......"* David was standing, arms folded, by the barrier. What premonitions did he have? And, then, at 18.15, April 4th, 2007, as I said, I met the man who was to mend my heart and break David's. There he was, in his too – small jacket and big red shoes, and I was lost. Gone for good at that moment.

"Oh HIIIIII!" I screeched.

"Hello," he said, in that honey voice and leant in to kiss my cheek.

"I'm David," said David, holding out his hand.

"Good journey? Train's on time. It's been sunny here today. Have you eaten? Would you like some tea somewhere? A café? Or a pint maybe? Are you tired?

Do you want to run away with me and keep me close in your heart in a place where no one will ever hurt us?"

I didn't actually say that last bit, but I WAS babbling like an idiot as we walked to the car. I don't remember the drive home, other than I had my hand on his foot all the way, like staking my claim, sneaking my fingers up his trouser leg, or maybe offering comfort. I could see him in the mirror too – and oh FUCK!! He's looking back! Blue eyes fixed on my reflection. I looked away, burned by the intensity of his stare.

We got home, had large gins. Dinner was ready. He'd changed and was wearing very loose pants, Indian style. He was somehow at my end of the table and – dear God - we were able to play footsie under the table. If David detected anything, he didn't show it. Dinner passed in a wine fuelled haze, and the next thing I know, Simon was lying (very provocatively, I have to say, you naughty man) on the settee, and I was right – he wasn't wearing any pants. And David made his move. I was horrified! Mine!! He's fucking MINE!!

The *'we don't play separately'* rule seemed cruelly inappropriate but there it was, so I had to join in and get what comfort I could. We went upstairs, I was drunk, and we had some sort of sex, the three of us, and after, went to bed. Me in the guest room, he in my bed. The only time that the stranger in my bed was welcome and I was in the next room.

The next day, we had a wander round town and then went to the beach and took a lot of photos in which, looking back at them now, there was such a clear and present connection between us; the way we stood, looked, posed, laughed, all pointed towards US being the couple and David the visitor.

Trebarwith, April 2004. Lovers. Big Red Boots.

We had drinks, overlooking the sea, and were joined by Paul, a sometime acquaintance and the man who was booked in for reiki the next day.

"Paul, this is Simon. He's a reiki master too, but is trained in Seichem. I'm Usui trained as you know. It might be good for you to have us both treat you tomorrow? What do you think?"

Paul agreed, and we went back home. I can't remember the evening. Did we do anything? I don't know, I was only enthralled to have this splendid man in my house and in my life, even just for a short while. It wasn't long before Simon went off to bed, early, on his own. I think he wanted to avoid another sex session, which he clearly hadn't enjoyed.

The next morning we did what ostensibly he had come down for and set ourselves up in the study to try to sort out the website, though it was clear all we wanted to do was to have sex again, on our own, but….*'we don't play separately'* and my luck was already massively pushed. We fiddled about with pictures and text frames and hyperlinks and CSS and made the best of it. Paul arrived at 2, and we began our reiki session. Paul had no idea of the cataclysm that was about to unfold above his head...

All was going well, Michael turned up on cue, I was treating Paul's neck, Simon his feet. The reiki filled the room and it was both tempestuous and healing. Then, I was bidden to stretch out my hand towards Simon, who did the same and our fingertips touched. I am not linguistically skilled enough to describe what then occurred – if you picture what may have passed between Adam and God, when their fingertips touched, as imagined in the ceiling of the Sistine Chapel. A bolt of pure energy exploded between us, through us, each into the other. It was terrifying, and powerful beyond words, but glorious and exultant and exhilarating and magnificent. We snatched our hands apart, both a bit stunned, like we'd been electrocuted by pure love, but unsure about what had just happened. When we eventually talked about it, after we'd stopped pretending it hadn't meant anything, it seemed a clear message from spirit that we had met our true soul mates; both open to spirit in that moment, we were able to transmit the true essence of each to the other. It was indefinable but without any room for doubt. We BOTH knew what had happened, but what the fuck to do about it? NOW what?

Even weirder, the next day David said:

"I'll do breakfast. Why don't you two go out for a walk? 20 minutes?"

"Erm, yeah, OK. You want to?"

"Sure, yeah," said Simon, glad to get me alone whenever he could.

So off we went, through the hedge, where John and I had wee'd so long ago, up to the Beacon; a bit of sightseeing always calmed things down a bit. There's a little area with picnic benches where you can sit and look far down West, where the eclipse had rolled up that day, back in '99, scaring the bejeesus out of us all. We sat. Opposite. Our hands touched and with no prompted thought I said:

"We're going to live in France, and I'm going to help you run a healing centre at your house. Aren't I?" Actually it wasn't a question, it was a fact, a thing I KNEW.

"Yes. We are," he said, and once more terrified, we leapt apart and said no more.

We went back to the house to finish the website (to sit really really close together). The site wasn't too bad; bit amateur really but it was by now, of course, completely irrelevant.

"I'm just going down the shop. I won't be long," called David, and out he went, leaving us alone. Again. Upstairs. *What the...?* I knew the shop, the local was just a few minutes and so there was no time to make love, not like we were both aching to do. So we kissed. Oh, how we kissed, deeply and completely. Like we would never part. My heart was racing, and my cock growing hard. I have not put that in gratuitously, dear readers; it is actually very relevant. It was getting hard and very visible in the green linen trousers I was wearing. Simon had no idea of the history, the torment, the sadness of my ED, and as he ran his fingers along the length of it, he smiled, and said, *"I am looking forward to when I can have that all for myself."*

"I love you," he said.

"I have HIV," I said.

BAM.

I hadn't planned to say anything. At least not yet. Not till we were somewhere safe, and he was mine, but that would have been absolutely the wrong thing. He needed to know before, so he had a chance to run. To be horrified. Disgusted. Afraid. Like I was.

There was a beat. A silence. And into it, I expected to hear the slamming of laptop lids, hurried excuses, eyes that were just a moment ago boring into mine, now downcast and avoiding meeting, business arrangements made to pay for the work done so far, 'Thanks, but no thanks'....

But not this man. Not this brave, gentle, honest, solid man.

He looked at me and said,

"That's OK, It doesn't matter. I love you. That's all that matters," and the front door opened and David was back. We sprang apart, erections wilting, red faced. What have I done? That's that then. Still better to know now than make some

stupid mistake and THEN have it go tits up. But I didn't know him, this man. This man of courage, this man who loved me. He meant what he said, and I had to trust it. But it wasn't mentioned again. Is that a good thing or a bad one?

That evening, we'd planned a meal, *en plein air*, round the chimenee, for which I was cooking Mexican. The works. I know it wasn't his last night, but we were planning to go out on the last night, a proper Cornish pub meal. I couldn't bear thinking about it, so I had some more gin. You KNOW what happens, Bray; you and gin are trouble. Anyway, I wanted to quell the panic of him leaving on Sunday. How would we ever put our plan into operation? Then, another weird thing: David said. *"Why don't you two go and have a walk before dinner? I'll do the prep?"* So off we went again. Alarming! What was he playing at? Trying? Trusting? Trapping? Dunno, but I just wanted out of the house, with Simon, for a wee while, probably for the last time, particularly now, after this morning's liddle revelation, before he left on Sunday.

We walked around the back lane to go up to the Beacon again. We sat on a little stone seat, and held hands and looked up as two jets left vapour trails...

X

it said. We climbed over the stile, walked up the field to the top and as the sun set over Treningle, my house, and my marriage, we held hands and knew, somehow, we were to be together.

"We'll have to wait, to find a way. I have NO idea how, or how long. But there will BE a way. YOU know what happened in that room," he said. The sun grew redder and the air cooler. *"Come on, let's go back. I'm bleddy starving!"* I said to steer the conversation away from the thing so huge it was uncontemplateable.

"We're back! Ready to eat everyone?"

I put ABBA on full blast, *('The Winner Takes It All')*, poured myself a glass of forget- me- juice and, watching David and Simon sitting chatting, through the window, began to cook dinner. All the red pepper pieces were the same size.

The Garden of Delights....

The tracks went down (*'Dancing Queen'* being caterwauled as I cooked), the wine went down and the sun went down. The chimenee was roaring, the table was set, the fajitas were done, the beans refried, the guacamole whizzed to a fine and spicy delight and....I wanted none of it. I wanted it all to go away, to be over and to be alone in Simon's arms. But. *"HEEEEERE we are!"* I yodelled, carrying out the food. We ate, the music played on, we talked about the inconsequential, the drinks went down.....then we ran out of chat and sat and watched the flames, mesmerised, in a row, with David in the middle.

Deliberate? Just how the chairs were? I don't know. What I DO know is that he was between us and, as I got more and more pissed, I got more and more desperate to touch Simon. What could I do? Lean across? Ask to swap seats? I know. I know - I'll just say, *"Excuse me, David, can I sit next to Simon as we'll be running away together soon."* Fortunately, Simon decided that he really didn't want to share me at bedtime again and excused himself and went to bed. Probably just as well; my gob was gearing up to run away with me, the pressure was so enormous.

"'Night....." Peck on my cheek as he leant in and I could smell him, feel his weight on my shoulder. *"'Night David,"* and he was gone. Leaving us together alone. I'm not sure why David suddenly started touching me, rubbing his hand up my thighs, proprietorially? As a reminder? Just horny? Whatever the reason, and I am ashamed to say, dear reader, that I found his touch offensive and wrong and I pushed his hand off. He put it back, nearer my cock this time and I said, *"Will you just fucking get off me!"* A little too fierce. A little too tell-tale. But, he did. Then he went and fetched the brandy (Dartington) decanter.

"I'm having a nightcap. I suppose you want one?" he said in that 'don't you think you've had enough already?' kind of voice.

"Yes, please, if that's alright. ... a bit more than THAT. If that's OK with you?" He'd poured enough to just make a film on the bottom of the (Dartington) glass. Remember, *I'M* in in control here..... *"Thank you.!* He poured more. "**More,** *if that's ok?"* By this time the glass was half full of neat brandy (Courvoisier) and we sat in silence, pretending that the flames were interesting. Actually they were. The brandy was fierce and I was becoming unmoored. The man I adored beyond all else was just 20 feet away, sleeping now no doubt, for now at peace and untroubled. More staring. More silence, as wide as the bed which now held my love.

"I've had enough of this. Shall we go to bed?"

"No, I'm fine. I'm staying for a bit. 'Night."

He picked up the decanter, in a meaningful way - I didn't care, I had enough left in the (Dartington) tumbler to drink myself unconscious.

"OK. Don't be long. And make sure the fire door's shut. And the water feature's switched off. And don't forget the light. And bring your glass in. I'm sure it'll be empty."

Go. Just go.

Alone and drunk, I wondered if he had any idea why I was so unhappy so suddenly? Everything was so exciting a couple of days ago. I supposed not, in a drunken kind of way; we'd done nothing untoward.

I heard a rustling from next door. Then I had a brilliant idea!

"Hey! I can hear you! And I can smell dope, you naughty girl! Roll us one?" Utter madness. A decision that could only be made by someone already robbed of sense and reason.

She passed the joint over the wall and I took a drag. Instantly my head began to spin and I felt disconnected from the world.

"Thanks, G".

"Go easy, you twat," came the whispered reply.

Another drag, further from reality. Another slug of brandy. And suddenly. Whoooo. Suddenly I was done. Enough already! I couldn't really see properly and standing was proving a bit tricky as everything was all slopey. I'm gonna slap that Barrie up him head for not laying this patio level. Ha, Golden Ear Whizz I'll give him. Hee heeeee heeeeee. Oh fuck. Suddenly my head spun really fast and I lost my balance, and toppled over, luckily landing on the steps by the gate and not the fire. Wait. Pause. Breathe. Breathe.

Everything slowly came back into focus and gingerly I tried to stand. Shut the fire door. 20 paces to the steps. Switch off water thing. 10 steps back to the door. Switch off light. Good boy I am. Fuckity arse. Forgot the glass. Ne'er mind eh? Need a pee now. Like NOW. Fortunately I had installed a handrail on the stairs. Came in handy as I hauled myself up to the loo, in that being really quiet drunk way. I had to pee like a girl as I'd have needed two hands to wee the boy's way and I had to hold on to the towel rail. Fuck, was I drunk. And stoned. The whole room was lurching and spinning as the THC in the cannabis thwhacked me in the brain. I felt AWFUL and sorrowful and regretful and my life was shit and nobody loved me and I needed some cheese. Yes, that was it. Cheese.

Hauling myself and then me drawers up, I felt my way back downstairs to the kitchen for cheese.

What was it again? I stared round the kitchen, swaying, and threatening to do that funny run that drunk people do, that we all laugh at when it's not you. I wanted….. um… I don't know now. My eyes stopped swivelling and came to rest on my phone, on the worktop. I moved towards it, oops, bit too fast, misjudged the distance there. I know! I'll write Simon a lovely text so he will see it in the morning when he wakes.

Now, as this is almost 8 years ago now, and given my condition at that time, this is from memory, but I think it's more or less what I wrote:

My darling Simon

You are sleeping not ten feet away and I am in the wrong bed. But don't worry because soon we will be in France together. I love you like I have never loved anyone else. It will be hard to say goodbye on Sunday, but it will only be temporary. I don't know how long, but be strong.

With all my heart. XXX

Aww, that's nice. He'll see that tomorrow. Bed. I now need sleep. Not cheese! That's what it was. Cheese, but I don't want cheese now I want bed. Not cheese. And I put my Samsung slider phone down on the top. And, before I ended up sleeping on the kitchen floor, wove my way back up the stairs to bed.

Leaving the phone on the bench, open. With the text unsent.

05.15. A time, easy to remember. Something kicked my foot, and startled me awake and I was facing the clock. That's how I know. Woahhhh my fucking head……sleep. More sleep. Then something kicked me again. I opened my eye, and swivelled it in the direction of where the pain was now coming from. And there was David. Holding my phone. Not really knowing what was happening, I raised myself, carefully onto one elbow – Jeez, brandy gives you the WORST hangover – and looked at him. What? What you just standing there for? What's that in your hand? What are you showing me? Focus. Focus. My phone. It's my phone.

"What?" What are you doing? Is that you kicking me?"

Silence.

"Why have you got my phone? Has somebody rung?"

"HOW LONG?"

"Uh? What? What are you saying?" Fog clearing....

"HOW FUCKING LONG?"

"What? How long what?"

"YOU AND HIM. HOW LONG HAS THIS BEEN FUCKING GOING ON????"

And he shoved my open phone in my face, where I could blearily discern *'My Darling Simon...'*. The beginning of the text I left on the work top. The one where I didn't press the 'send' key. Oh my days. You know the feeling when you are utterly busted, completely fucked with no possible recourse or excuse? That moment when the blood drains from all your vital organs, and leaves you with no breath, just a feeling of imminent death? That's what I had and realising that there really WAS no way out, said:

"Three days. That's all. Three days". That was kind of true, but not really, as it had been going on for weeks, even months or even years if you factor in the time the planets have been spinning and bringing us to this moment.

"Down fucking stairs. Now." David rarely swore, so I think he was prolly a bit mad at this point. I stumbled out of bed, feeling real bad. Really sick, hungover, tired, but not scared. That was the remarkable thing. This could have been a trigger for all those times my Dad had thrashed me, but this time I didn't care. I was SO clear in my intentions, he could do or say what he liked – it just WAS.

He was standing silhouetted in the window, the orange halo making his features indiscernible

"Three days? THREE FUCKING DAYS AND YOU'RE GOING TO FRANCE?"

"Yes."

"How? Where will you live? What on? You don't have any money."

That much was true. I HAD money, but never had any access to it. He always managed the money; when we went shopping for Stuff, he always paid; when we ate out, he always paid. He always joked: *"he's like the Queen – never carries any money. Ha hahaa"* Yes, you control freak. That's because you never let me have any. And again, I let it happen. So. Not really your fault. Mine. Stupid mine, which has led me, finally, to this moment.

"How will you get there? You don't even know him. Are you fucking mad?"

"I don't know how. Or why, or when. All I DO know is that I love him and I WILL be leaving you. For him. Sorry. But that's just the truth."

"He won't love you. Not like I do. Anyway you've got AIDS."

And that, dear reader, was the end of all things. If Simon had left tomorrow alone, there is now no way I could ever stay here with this man, who had just said the cruellest of things. I had never fully recovered from, or forgiven him for, the Monstrous Lie, but had married him anyway, but that, *that* was the worst thing he could possibly have said. And it was the end.

"*Sorry. Nothing else I can say.*" Actually there was, but noticing the clenching fists and increase in breathing decided it was in the interests of self-preservation that I didn't. I just sat, naked and shivering – cold, post adrenalin, fear, all three – on the settee that had seen so many betrayals and waited.

*"WELL HE CAN FUCK OFF. FUCK OFF OUT OF MY HOUSE NOW!! GO AND WAKE HIM UP! AND YOU! YOU FUCK OFF WITH HIM! BOTH OFF YOU! FUCK OFF!! **FUCK OFF OUT OF MY HOUSE!!!!**"*

I thought about reminding him it was OUR house, actually, but given the circs....

So I went back upstairs, found my clothes from where I'd stumbled out of them earlier, and went in next door. The room of more betrayals.

"Simon," I whispered, "*Wake up. Wake **up***."

"*Gnnnnnnn….. Oh, good morning. Why's it still dark? What time is it?*"

"It's early. Come on, get up. We have to go."

"Go where? What's wrong?"

I'll tell you as we go. Just get up. Can we go to yours? In London?"

"Uh…."

"Here's the phone. Ring your landlady and ask. Do it now."

He sat up, this man to whom I was now committed and was risking everything for, rubbed his eyes, and said, *"Has something happened?"* Somewhat of an understatement…..

"Just ring home and see if I can stay for a couple of days. We have to leave. Now."

After a muffled conversation, which I only heard through the bathroom wall from where I had gone to collect stuff, he said, *"She says it's OK. Are you going to tell me what's happened?"*

"David knows about us. I'll explain as we go. I have to get a cab. Pack your stuff. Hello? Bodmin Taxis? Yes, Parkway please. Immediately. Thankyou. I'll see you downstairs."

"I need my Barclaycard."

"Please."

"My card. I need it. There's a cab coming."

No response. Just a back, implacably turned towards me. My card was on the worktop. I picked it up. *"OK. Well"*

"I'll see you then."

Simon came down the stairs and I herded him, dazed and confused, straight out of the front door, and into the waiting cab, driven by, irony of ironies, Mr. Nigel Spank Me. There's always humour in the blackest places, eh?

On the way to the station I explained about the text and what happened after, and you know what? He just said: *"Well, there you go. Reiki has a funny way of working, but work it does…"*

We were in a bit of a state of shock – I had no idea what would happen now; we were together; it was out in the open; I had no Plan B, But, after a strong coffee and politely telling a well-meaning, but really really annoying man to FUCK OFF and no, we weren't interested in seeing his model railway, we boarded the 08.20 to Paddington, holding hands all the way to London, as we hurtled towards whatever new life awaited us.

CHAPTER ELEVEN.

MORE UPS AND DOWNS THAN A WHORE'S DRAWERS.

<u>In which our hero goes back and forth and round and round and up and down, walks the red carpet and builds a blanket fort.</u>

'500 Miles'.

by The Proclaimers. No.1 April 7th 2007.

The distance doesn't matter. I'll always come back home to you.

~ ~ ~

The train hurtled on, to a strange land, with strange folk in it. I knew nobody, nor where I was headed, but I knew, as I stole a sideways glance at Simon, who had dozed off, that wherever and whatever befell me, with this man beside me, I could slay the dragons and wraiths that might rise up against me. I had a feeling of absolute trust in him, as if I had known him all my life, and I guess I probably had; I just hadn't met him yet. Plymouth, Exeter, Bristol, Totnes, Reading – further and further from the familiarity of the past 17 years, but with a murmuring of joy in my gut. Then, bustling Paddington. After telling a most elegant (and shocked, but delighted) woman that I thought she was beautiful and very elegant, we stopped for a coffee at Ritazza, on the concourse, which became a point of reference for us, the kind of place where lovers met, affairs were designed, partings were wrenched….there we were, all alone, fresh canvases to write our new lives upon. Tube, bus, rush, tube, no time to really absorb was what happening.

We came out of the station, and I, exhilarated, said, in a kind of Vivien Leigh way, returning to Tara:

"I am never going to let anybody tell me what to do, ever again!"

And Simon, above the roar of buses and honking of cabs, turned his beautiful blue eyes to me, and said, *"I won't,"* and so it was.

Eventually we arrived at Simon's house, or rather his digs, and let ourselves in and sank gratefully onto the settee in the lounge. Where we fell on each other, like two lovestarved orphans, and yes – erections burgeoning. Things were becoming clearer in my mind, about cause and effect…. Anyway we snogged and snogged and fondled a bit, like teenagers, wary of an interruption, which came not very long after, and quelled our ardour fairly sharpish.

"Um, hello Wendy. This is…um…this is Nigel. Is it OK if he stays for a couple of days?"

"Hello, Wendy. Thankyou."

"Yes, that'll be fine. Simon we need some shopping. Will you go please?"

"Yes, of course. The usual?"

"Yes. Don't be long now."

I found myself outside again, then in the car, then in Tesco, doing the shopping. This was getting more surreal by the moment.

"Why are you doing the shopping? By the look of it, they've just BEEN shopping…."

"Oh, I always do it," was all the explanation I got.

Sainsbury's was the first place, over a bunch of coriander, I called him 'Si'.

We stopped for a pint afterwards, in the April sun. I just stared at him, just couldn't stop staring at this man, who had saved my life. Astonishing to think that this time, 24 hours ago, we were on the Beacon in Bodmin…..in the blink of an eye, my life had changed. I was not naïve enough to forget I'd be going back soon, and what I would face there I didn't know, but for now, the beer was cold, the sun was warm and the man across the table was utterly astonishing to me.

"They don't seem to have any. Don't worry. I'll ask.."

"No don't! Oh god….."

"It'll be fine."

We were in a chemist, on our way home.

"Excuse me? Hello?" Stop chewing your HubbaBubba and serve me?

"Ah, yes I can't see any here. Do you have any extra-large condoms, please?"

Ha! That stopped her chewing! She went 'out the back', and asked. Si was hopping from foot to foot, with embarrassment. Or maybe anticipation? Anyway, she came back with some, wordless and gum-filled and handed them over, stuck her hand out, and I paid. ME! I actually paid. Myself! With *MY* money.

We went back to the house with the shopping, and had some food (which Si cooked) and said some things to some people and then excused ourselves and went upstairs. It was the most thrilling / strange thing. Strange, as I was now alone with him, with nobody to tell me to stop, nobody to shame me, nobody to make me feel guilty, because you know what, dear reader? I felt no shame. No guilt. I had left my husband (CIVIL PARTNER!!!) just that morning, and I could barely remember his face, and nor did I want to. I knew, without any doubt that I was in the right place, that I had waited my entire life for this moment and what would follow from it. Reiki does indeed work in mysterious ways. This was no accident! The timing was perfect. I'd *had* to go to Hungary – a time of shriving; to Germany – a time of coming to understand the kind of life I did *not* want; to get married to understand finally where I SHOULD be. In the heart of *this* man. My HIV, Anna, Hartley, *IS* a gift, for without it I would never have had to face my mortality, face the demons of my Father, face my place in the world as a gay man. You were right, as you knew you would be so proved.

I AM GAY.

I AM A GAY MAN.

I AM A GOOD PERSON.

I HAVE WORTH.

I HAVE LOVE AND GIVE IT FREELY.

I AM A GAY MAN.

It had taken me 51 years to be able to say this and know it be true. And it was thanks to this extraordinary person beside me.

So we sat, on the bed, cross legged, just looking at each other and then dissolved into each other's soulplace and made love with such intensity of spirit it was utterly astonishing. And when we came, and yes, I did, with no problem whatever, it was with such an outpouring of our very selves nothing would ever be the same again. For either of us.

Just for today, do not worry.

Just for today, do not anger.

Honour your parents, teachers and elders.

Earn your living honestly.

Show gratitude to everything.

Mikao Usui.

In that moment, I had achieved half.

The four days passed in a blur of lovemaking, tenderly, sweetly, sometimes just shagging with gay abandon (see what I did there?), cooking, and….film making! Oh yes! My man was making a film about the murder of gays in Iraq; not a cheerful subject but nevertheless….Peter Tatchell was involved and Si had been to interview him. Silly tart that I am, I was all star struck and wide eyed so when he said on the Sunday he had to go to the studio to do the final edit, I was well made up. Actually it was boring as bat shit as the producer was such a pedant, nothing actually got done. Still it was interesting and I anyway, I didn't care cos I was wiv mah man! I wandered off half way through and went to find a café, sitting under the trees, a tall glass of cold Staropramen, full of such joy and fresh air, hardly knowing who I was…..and trying desperately hard not to think about what was to come…..

…but come it did, and Si came to Paddington with me and it was one of those *'Brief Encounter'* moments although I don't recall either Celia Johnson or Trevor Howard actually sobbing as the train pulled out along the station, but, fuck stiff upper lips! ….we cried and we held hands for as long as we were able until the speed pulled us apart.

Reading, Totnes, Exeter, Plymouth, Saltash, Liskeard, Bodmin and here we are, drab, empty, with David waiting as he agreed to come and pick me up. Don't ask.

The following week was bizarre; David carried on as if nothing had happened. We ate together, watched telly, went shopping. I don't think we saw anyone – too many awkward questions – but it was if I'd just been away for a couple of days. (further than anyone could possibly know). Except. We both knew it had happened and we both knew it would never go back to how it was and I was now sleeping in the spare room. Awkward. Simon was ringing every night and we'd have long chats, which must have been very difficult but – but, you started this, so…..

"What shall I tell Gaynor?"

Tell her you've got a job and you're going away for a while."

"Why don't I just tell her the truth?"

"Because you won't have to live with her crying and moaning will you? You'll tell her what I said."

Lies again. Secrets and lies. Deceive my besty. Your fabrications had already lost you any respect I'd ever had for you and now you're asking me do it again!!! But I did. I was so conditioned to do as I was told, I just acquiesced. As always. Beagle boy.

"Hey Gaynor! Guess what! News! I've got news! Can I come over?"

So, we sat in the garden and looking at, or trying to, my best friend I said:

"You know that Simon, that was here? Well, he's got a place in France and a business, and he's offered me a teaching job! Teaching English!"

"Where?"

"In France, you twat!"

"Oh. Don't call me fookin twat, you twat. That's brilliant. How long for?"

"Erm, not sure…about six months I think." How the lies poured off my tongue…

"Aww, that's grand. I'll miss you, but you'll have lots of stories when you get back! Well done!" and she got up to give me one of her Power Hugs that squeezed the air from your lungs and realigned your ribs. "*Let's have wine to celebrate!*" 'When you get back' skewered me to the floor.

And so we drank, toasting my duplicity, to my dishonouring of our friendship and to another lie in the web of deceit I had become part of, while my friend was happy for me. This caused massive harm when she found out later; she was hurt, and angry and unforgiving. And still I didn't betray David. I took all her wrath and pain squarely on the chin. It wasn't until much later she found out and switched the source of her anger to the perpetrator and apologised unreservedly to me. But I was as much to blame – I had been weak. I should have said no, and told her. But the abused never stand up, do they?

One night, during one of our late night calls, a propos of nothing, Si said *'We're going to France for a week! Meet you in Ritazzas tomorrow!"* Just like that! And there I was, back on the train – Liskeard, Plymouth, Exeter, Totnes, Reading, Paddington, his arms. Boom. Coffee at our favourite table and then into the West End because Si had to go home to pay his rent, so we had tea in the Charing Cross Hotel. Very naice. Si went off, I fiddled on my laptop till he came back. It was delightful. It was elegant. It was fucking £38.75! For a cup of tea, two coffees and a tiddly cake? Never mind. New life. Stop moaning....

Train to Stansted, bleddy ansum pasty from The Cornish Pasty Company stall on Liverpool Street station (you can take the boy out of Cornwall...), flight to Tours, hire car and driving in to the night to the place that was to become my home.

It was utterly black when we arrived. The roads from the city had got smaller and smaller and now we turned into a single track road, and pulled up in front of the house. Well, I say 'house'. After we had managed to get through the six foot high grass and weeds, unsnagged ourselves from the brambles, we opened the front door to find the place all stinky and damp, full of cobwebs and dust. And I loved it. Si said he'd brought his former partners here both of whom had said, *"WHAT THE......???"* and he was worried I'd say the same. I didn't, much to his relief, and anyway the die was pretty much cast and I'd have lived in a cardboard box with him, if that's all he had. The place had been locked up for weeks and the cleaners Si had paid clearly hadn't been near the place.

"Bed, eh?" said Si. *"Long day."*

"Can we go to the garden first?"

"It'll be like a jungle, but…..ok then."

There was a torch and we struggled through the undergrowth to the Big Oak. I wrapped my arms round it and in that moment knew I'd come home.

We slept on the rickety old bed like babes, lost in the woods, which we were, pretty much.

The next morning we had a bath, in the bedroom, where there a huge corner bath (handy) and went to town to get some food. 'Foreign shopping' wasn't a problem for me, of course so we just got what we could afford and hunkered down. The week slipped by so smooth, so fast, so full of love and anticipation and then it was the last night and we ate cheese and drank wine and danced together by the single bulb. I quote this here in full because it is OUR song, it is what we danced to, holding each other close, full of wonder and because it says exactly what Simon has done for me:

You've got a way with me
Somehow you got me to believe
In everything that I could be
I've gotta say-you really got a way

You've got a way it seems
You gave me faith to find my dreams
You'll never know just what that means
Can't you see, you got a way with me

It's in the way you want me
It's in the way you hold me
The way you show me just what love's made of
It's in the way we make love

You've got a way with words
You get me smiling even when it hurts
There's no way to measure what your love is worth
I can't believe the way you get through to me

It's in the way you want me
It's in the way you hold me
The way you show me just what love's made of
It's in the way we make love

Oh, how I adore you, Like no one before you

I love you just the way you are

It's in the way you want me
Oh it's in the way you hold me
The way you show me just what love's made of
It's in the way we make love
It's just the way you are.

Shania Twain. 'You've Got A Way' lyrics © Universal Music Publishing Group

But again, the time came to face the reality of other people's judgement and scorn and bitterness but I felt much stronger now, invincible in fact, immune to the arrows and slings that were to come my way. By now of course the word was out. When I got back…. Reading, Totnes, Exeter, Plymouth, Saltash, Liskeard, Bodmin….David picked me up (again!), my phone was very busy. *'Is it true?' 'Oh no! Not you two! You're perfect for each other!' 'What happened? Never mind, you'll sort it out'*….if only they knew; a mismatch if ever there was one, and I HAD sorted it out thank you very much. Me and my 'whim' were leaving.

Si, in the honest and admirable way that he has, had agreed to work out his months' notice on his rent and do some decorating, so we had seventeen days to be apart. Actually that was 17 years, or that's how it felt, anyway. I had a long standing arrangement to house sit for Anna's dogs and it fell in the middle of this period so at least I was out of the house and David didn't have to suffer the agonies of nightly calls (though by this time, he had a new squeeze of his own and was doing the same thing, which didn't hurt exactly but was just weird. Like the time in a threesome, he was fucking the other bloke – I didn't care, it was just…weird.) and so we could talk long into the night.

We didn't have phone sex, (well, maybe once or twice) we had phone *love*. Stop sniggering at the back. It's true. We used to just chat and plan and eventually one of us would talk the other to sleep….I'd hear his breathing change and slow and he'd stop replying and I knew he'd be gone, drifted away from the day…. And then the phone would go again in the morning and there he'd be, all bright and washed with sleep. I had the joy of walking the dogs, the joy of pleasing myself and the joy of knowing it was 17…..16….15…days to go.

CATASTROPHE!! Si has just told me he's got the date for the premier of his film, in London and he's asked me to go...and I'm at fucking ANNA'S!! But, riding to the rescue came my old mate Marion (is there a joke there?) who I'd known since the day I got the job at the school we both went for back in '88.

"Maz!! What can I do? I HAVE to get to London..."

"Stop flapping! Tell me what's wrong..."

I did, breathlessly.

"Oh don't worry. Come and pick me up, and I'll cover for you. Its only one night. Get the early train, and then I'll come and get you from 'Droof station the next day."

"Yes but, what if....."

"Stop being a poof. I said I'll do it. Nobody'll be any the wiser." Although of course they were, because she told her husband who told my husband, who of course is a very close friend of Anna's......I don't know to this day if she knows or not. I suspect she does, but the dogs were fine, the house wasn't robbed by the stranger, so I guess she figured it didn't matter.

And so it came to pass. On the train again – up and down, up and down – Redruth, St. Austell, Bodmin, Liskeard, Saltash, Plymouth, Exeter, Totnes, Reading....know the route yet? And there he was, fawn linen jacket, new trousers, sexy as.

"Coffee?"

"Yes I think so".

"Ritazza?"

"I think so."

"Thanks for coming."

"I love you".

RItazza Café, Paddington. Thrills and Sorrows.

Off to the Horse Hospital which was built in 1797 as stabling for cabby's sick horses. The Horse Hospital is now a unique Grade II listed arts venue situated in an unspoilt mews in the heart of Bloomsbury, and it is a really amazing building, with special knobbly floors to stop the horses slipping. So, there we were, a crowd of earnest film enthusiasts, queer activists, lezzers and intellectuals all here to see my man's film. I was SO proud. He introduced me all round as 'my partner, and I was happy to bask in the glow of his success. It was a short film, harrowing and very powerful and evoked much discussion and lit fires. After, we got a Subway thingy (oooh! the glamour of the film world) and a cab and then a train back to Wendy's who was not very pleased to see me as of course I was the reason her houseboy and servant was leaving. SO, another long night of joy and love making, and we slept until the alarm went at stupid o'clock and I set off back to the station, all big and grown up, on my own!

Paddington, Reading, Totnes, Exeter, etc etc back down to Redruth where Maz was waiting, and back to the house. Job done. No more trains now, eh?

And so came the last few days at 'home' – the marks are necessary, because it wasn't home now; it was just a place I was sleeping until I could leave. As Rose Royce once said: *"Love don't live here anymore"*……well not for me.

I need to explain a bit here, I think, in case *you're* thinking I'm just a heartless cunt. Well, I'm not. To quote Anne Lamott:

"You own everything that happened to you.

Tell your stories.

If people wanted you to write warmly about them,

they should've behaved better."

This story is how *I* remember it, and how *I* see it. Others can (and certainly did) see it differently but all I can say is 'You were not living inside it and so you really have no right to judge it, or me'. I, without realising, so gradual was it, had allowed myself to be owned, controlled and manipulated. David had replaced my Father and I liked that because he loved me and didn't loathe me, but I hated it too, as he always made me feel stupid, inferior and small. Not unkindly, not with malice, but nevertheless, he did. I had been stolen. All my choices were not actual choices, all the decisions I had made were not really mine. And so when I found an alternative universe (which I had forgotten even existed) in which there was a man who loved me unconditionally, was fair and gentle, interested in equality and justice, and was not interested in playing power games, why *wouldn't* I choose option B? Yes, of course it was hard, it was painful, it was frightening – I hadn't been in the outside world for 17 years; I had forgotten how to do things for myself and it was terrifying and thrilling in equal measure. There was always going to be collateral damage and leaving the country I'm sure lessened the impact.

In the midst of this sea of sorrows, I went to see Anna, as I didn't know how to proceed. Maybe SHE, with her clear eye and bullshit detector would have something to say that would guide me through. I knew what I wanted, what was right, but didn't know the *how* of it. She as always, made sense of the turmoil. It was like the last hurrah!, where I could weep out all the pain – the pain of separation, the pain of anger having realised I had been duped for all those years; it was like having been kept in a cellar for years and then suddenly someone had prised off the coal cover. And light had flooded in. It was just the *sadness* of it all. Through the snot and the tears, aware of the deep and abiding friendship she had with him, I snivelled:

"But I've really hurt him."

"That's none of your business."

"What? But...."

"No. It isn't. How he feels is none of your business."

Quite a concept to get my head round.

"But the house. There's a mortgage."

"Sell it."

"I can't, it's his home"

"Yes. You CAN. You may not want to, but you CAN. He'll have to find another home."

"But what about all my stuff – we bought it together."

"Leave it. Why would you want to take your old stuff to a new life?"

And that, dear reader, is what I did. In a stroke, Anna (and Jophiel, who was surely there, speaking the truth) cleansed me and healed me.

And THAT is why I was able to leave so calmly, looking outward and toward the man who had come to save me. And *not* because I was a heartless cunt.

That too, was the end of the extremely deep and complex relationship with Anna, a woman of exceptional power and wisdom. We'd met, we'd loved, she'd done what she was supposed to have done, and we moved through. So, thank you Anna, for more than you could ever know. Oh, but wait – of course you do! Medicine Woman, Sage, Healer, - I thank you profoundly for the difference you made.

I told David I was going to stay with Debs for the weekend; the house was unbearable now, with an air of impending doom. I packed as much as I could carry, in two suitcases, while David, mute as stone, looked on. I felt powerful, I felt open, I knew that long stored reiki was working for me and that my empowerment was not going to fail. My sister, bless her (karma) had said we could have her little house and that's what we planned. As the days shrank down from 17, 16, 15,….I felt calm, right and ready. This time I thought it unsympathetic to ask for a lift to the station but still, David drove me, not a word was spoken and he left me waiting for the train West. Then, did I mention, Si came too? We had an amazing weekend, full of sun and laughter, beer and sex and it was over too soon, but it was OK because it was just a break, an interlude, an *entre'act*, before the final scenes were to be played out he was going back to get his stuff and then, soon….

We were back at the station waving him off, crying just a bit, and then we sat in the car to have a calm-down fag. My phone went and I texted back, something about waiting to go to the clinic, which was the next item on the day's agenda, after dropping Deb' off, and making some excuse, before beer. Then I had a panic and said to Debs:

"Fuck I thought I'd mentioned the HIV clinic then by accident. I don't want HER to know my status! It's alright, I checked back and I'd just said we're in Truro, that's all."

There was a horrible silence and then Debs said,

"What status?"

Oh. Oh fuck. Fuckkety fuck. Busted. So I took a (very) deep breath and said,

"I'm HIV positive." It dropped like a bomb in to the silence.

"OK, erm…Cool," she said. There wasn't much else to say really.

Again, with hindsight lending depth and purpose, the fact that nobody ever mentioned it became a 'good thing' – it normalised it; people didn't seem worried for me, scared of me and thought it wasn't even really relevant to my everyday, healthy life

Hazel and size $8^{1/2}$.

CHAPTER TWELVE.

THE SUMMER OF LURVE.

<u>In which our hero finds the boy again, makes peace with the Devil, and puts himself out of harm's way.</u>

'Signal Fire'.

by Snow Patrol. No.7, 28th April 2007.

I have no fear when you are there, standing in front of me.

~ ~ ~

I had stayed with Debbie the night before, and Si was due the day after. I borrowed Debs' car and went to meet him. Way too early, of course and found myself, in an all too familiar way, *skipping about like a gurl* only this time David wasn't there, oozing disapproval.

Could be, who knows? There's something due any day

I would know right away soon as it shows

It may come cannon balling down through the sky

Gleam in its eye, bright as a rose

Who knows? It's only just out of reach

Down the block on a beach under a tree

I got a feeling there's a miracle due

Gonna come true, coming to me......

This breathless lyric from *West Side Story* sums up the nervous nearly pooin-me-pants excitement, knowing he was on the train and with every clickety clack he was nearer...

…..heart racing, skipping to and fro….being 45 minutes early wasn't a good idea…..

...text: *'Bodmin'* (Oh the irony).

...text: *'Lostwhithiel'*

...text: *'St Austell'*

...text: *'Stuck in St Austell'* Oh FFS!!!

...text: *'Left St.Austell'*….

...text: *'Truro next stop'*...

And. There he was. Right there. Hot, tired but there. I swear it was a runn –y thing, along the station in slow mo, into each other's arms. It was hard to believe as it goes, as for the first time so far, there was nobody else telling us what to do, how to be, where to go, judging, criticising, analysing...just us, and the choice to be just how we wanted. And at that moment, it was in bed. My desire for him was overwhelming; not in a pervy, shaggy kind of (well, maybe a bit) but in the way of needing to have a singular intimate connection where nobody could interfere or make us feel that it was wrong. Because it wasn't.

We drove back to Falmouth to let the party of all parties begin. Summer 2007.

We had arranged to meet Gill in town the next day and so we walked down to the City centre and there was my beautiful sister, waiting, a bit nervously, but of course, Si just hugged her and squeezed it all away. He does that, you know. We had a cold beer in the warm sun and everything was perfect. As Si hadn't been to Truro before, we had a little walk round and apparently, unknown to me at the time, in the cathedral with its slanting light and silent air, Gill had taken Si to one side, and said:

"Mum asked me to look after him. Well, now it's your turn and I hand him into your care." Nice, eh?

We went back to Gill's little cottage and when I say *little*…..we decided we were going to fuck in the shower but after me getting trapped in the door and Si repeatedly banging his head on the shower head, we decided maybe it was a bit *too* small.

"Bedroom, then," he said.

We began again, tenderly, slowly, silently, apart from our breath. After some time he said,

"I want to fuck you now. Join with you."

"Where are the condoms?"

"We don't need them anymore," and with that and with infinite care he slid into me, making a connection so deep, so intense I thought my heart would burst. I sobbed, I think, with a joy so complete, so grateful, so overwhelming, and he said, *"Did I hurt you?"*

"No," I sobbed, *"No. You just wiped all the hurt away."* I didn't need to explain that. He knew of my trauma with my status, my, shame, my fear and with that one, unselfish act, cancelled out months of agony and self-hatred.

"I've been doing my homework, you know. I've read all the reports and data and studies. I know you've been undetectable for years now, and the risk of infection is negligible. And it IS just a risk, and I wanted to show you how deeply I love you". And I sobbed myself to sleep in his arms. He smelled of soap and sweat.

After, we decided to gatecrash the party at Debs' so we got dressed, got a cab, got some beverages and arrived at Gylling Street. Where we stayed for the next three months. There was room there, there was energy, and most importantly it was in the centre of town. I felt bad after Gill had been so generous, but there just wasn't room – we had two huge suitcases each and no transport. It just made sense, though I knew she was pissed off with me. I hope she knows it was nothing personal. The pasty shop and Threshers the Offy were within sight of the flat. No contest.

The Summer was golden, hilarious and full of possibility. You know that feeling of terror/joy when it's all brand new and sparkly? Everything is wonderful and nothing is impossible? There were always people turning up, always fun to be had and as the Summer wore on, the hurts and the fears were gently smoothed away, by the sun, the sea and his love for me.

Happy happy!

Debs said we could stay on the blow up mattress that first night as there were still people occupying the beds from the weekend. We blew it up and lay it in front of the fireplace, and stumbled to bed. I was on the fireplace side and Si, being a big lad, said he'd have the other side. So, he flopped down on the bed, catapulting me up into the air and into the grate. When we'd finally stopped laughing we decided to drive back to Gill's and come back the next day.

Debs had a friend who had a thing about Russian gymnasts and it became a Thing, and it developed and we decided that he was called Boris and he lived under the bed in the spare room, useful for housework. And stuff. One day we had a party on the balcony and I decided it was time to meet him. We also had been designing a new recipe book on ways to serve saffron cake, and we had one in the kitchen. Without a thought, I stripped off completely, put on an apron and a Russian accent, and carrying a plate of 'saffron cubes dressed with tomato wedges and chocolate', Boris appeared on the balcony, stark bollock naked, apart from the apron.

"*Cake,*" he said. "*I vant you try cake. Iss very good.*"

The reactions were mixed and priceless.

"*Mummy!! MUMMY!*" said Debs' daughter. "*I can see Uncle Nigel's bum!!*" and she shrieked with delight.

Debs was unable to speak for laughing, that great deep laugh that shakes your soul and renders you helpless.

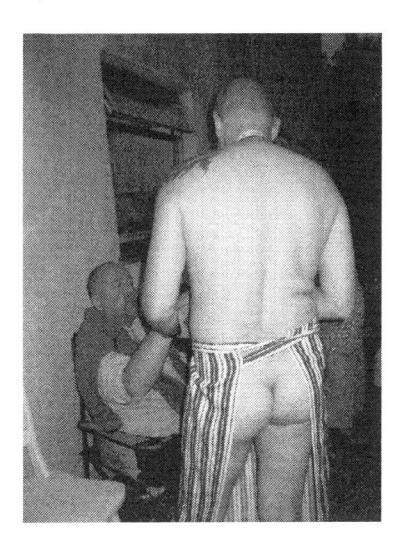

Boris. And his arse.

Debs' straight friend backed in to the corner, as Boris closed in, insisting he had enough cake already, terrified and alone as Debs was no use to anyone.

Si was…..well…both astonished and delighted. He loved this man-child, this man who would do this with such aplomb! He stared in wonder and joy that I was his. His. And I was so happy because I would never *NEVER* have done such a thing before, and had never been as free spirited in nine'teen years. It was a revelation and a source of undiluted joy.

Eyebrows were raised, pretend laughs were guffawed and Boris just continued to serve, showing his bare arse to everyone, not needing approval or permission from anyone. *"Have cake. Iss nice."*

Wot Larks, eh Pip?

It was wonderful day, as were all the days that summer. My birthday came and we celebrated all day, got kicked out of the bar we were in, tried to blag our way into a concert without tickets, went skinny dipping, me and Debs

We coulda drowned!

Then fireworks, drunk as skunks, which whizzed and screamed by as they weren't set off properly or safely – shades of Bremen! – then happily to bed , at the start of another brand new year with my brand new love. The thought that we were leaving for France soon made the end of that day, month, all the more special and important.

Unfinished business.

There was the only one thing that clouded that blue skied summer. And I needed to resolve it and reach an end. I went to face my Nemesis.

"Hi."

"Oh 'ello boy. I didn't know you were coming. Where's David?"

"Can I come in please, I need to talk to you?"

He sat in the grease stained, fag scented armchair and I stood by the fire place.

"He's not here. We've split up." Beat. *"I'm with somebody else now. His name is Simon. And we're living in Falmouth."*

"Awww, no. That's a pity. I liked 'ee. 'Ee was a good ole boy. What're ee doin' in Falmouth?"

"Staying with Debs for a while. Then I'm moving to France. With Simon. Maybe to teach English. I don't know yet. But there are somethings I need to say before I leave." I was aware that this actually could be the last time I saw him, not that I cared, but there was something unavoidable to be done.

"What're goin' to live on? Got any money 'ave ee?"

"No. Well, not much. That's not why I'm here. Just sit down and don't say anything till I'm finished, OK?

I took a deep breath, no longer afraid of this little man sat before me, opened my mouth and said all the things I had waited years, *years*, to say:

I want you to know that I don't **care** *what you think of my lifestyle, whatever that's supposed to be. I know you find it foul, that you say disgusting things to Gill and Barrie – they tell me, you know… NO!* **DON'T** *interrupt. I know all you think of is me being in the Shit Shovers Union, as you so hurtfully put it, but I am more than that. I am a good man. I was a good teacher, I am a good son, I am a good partner. I am considerate, and loyal and caring and loving. I work hard, I pay my bills. In fact I am just like you. Only nicer.*

I was now in full spate, this speech, rehearsed so many times over the years, now just flooding forth…still measured, still calm, still in control of what I was saying. No fear of this man, who had beaten me, betrayed me, belittled me.

"But. I need you to know that I understand why you are so bigoted, so hateful, so ashamed. Given the vile spiteful woman who brought you up, so embittered and full of rage herself, I am not surprised that you deal with anything you don't understand or approve of by being hateful and vengeful yourself. I get it. I do.

I know what you say about me. I know you lie to your friends because you're too ashamed to have a gay son, that you tell them I'm a headmaster! That's just a lie. Why do you SAY that? It's just not true! You spread poison and lies about each of us to the others – do you think we don't talk to each other? That we don't know what you've said about each of us?

I was watching him, so small, so transfixed. Why was I ever afraid of him?

I know your Father left you when you were a baby; he was in South Africa when you were only four. I know you were brought up by an embittered and angry woman. I don't know what that did to you, or being a member of that insane Methodist chapel, but all of these things conspired to make you like you are and to take YOUR bitterness out on an easy target – your 'queer poof of a son'. Especially when he's not around to defend himself.

*Well, I am here to say only this. I will NEVER forgive you, or forget, the hurts and damage you heaped upon my sisters and the years of hell you put my mother through. But those are not mine to forgive, I suppose. That is up to them, and now Mum is dead and no longer part of the misery you cause. Still cause...But for me I can say only this: One - I no longer care what you think. I know my worth to the world, to my friends and my partner and, two – I forgive you. Forgive you for the undeserved beatings, all the hurt and rejection, the shame you made me feel, the self-loathing you made me feel and the desertedness you made me feel. Because I really don't think it was, at heart, your fault. You didn't stand a chance. But you **could've** made a choice. A choice not to judge me, not to loathe me but to accept me, love me and be proud of my achievements. But you didn't.*

I just want you to know it doesn't matter now. I'm done."

Tears were threatening, my pitch was rising. I was spent. All those years of need spat forth and I felt cleansed. Purged. He was just watching, like I wasn't even speaking. Then, do you know what he said?

"*You'll need some money if you're going to set up a school in France. You can have your inheritance early. I treat all you kids the same* (biting of tongue in incredulity) *so how much do you need?"*

Did you just **hear** anything I said? Were you even **listening**? Or did you hear and for once you were found out? Or was this an attempt to buy me off? Get rid of me? Get me right out of the country – to never need to see your abomination again? Give me money to make up for all the years of hurt? Well, you know what? Fuck it. I don't CARE why, and anyway, I knew better to listen to what he said – I had the real version from my siblings.

"Yes, if you're offering," I said. *I'm sure the others will have something to say, believe I coerced you, but they weren't here, were they? They didn't hear this conversation. They can believe what they like. How much are you thinking?"*

"I can give you £5000 if that will do? That's your share."

"Really? Well, yes, that should be plenty to get me started. Thankyou." And so for the next five days, I travelled over to Truro and he withdrew £1000 a day. Blood money. And I felt not the least bit guilty: he offered, I accepted.

On the last day, he said, *"I would like to buy you and your Friend lunch."* Capital F. After my initial astonishment, given that he didn't speak to David for nearly eight years, I thanked him and the following day, we met. In the British Legion. All Day Breakfast. Congealed bacon and eggs. Classy. But the thought was there, and he met Simon. He kept calling him David, but they got on OK. Maybe he HAD heard some of what I'd said? Who knows? We went to a pub after, where I bought the drinks as he said they were too expensive and he refused to pay that much, after which I went to fetch the car. I arranged to meet them at the main roundabout in town. When I arrived, he saw the car and just dragged Si out in to the middle of the traffic, which was swerving round them, tyres screeching, horns blaring until I managed to pull up, in the middle of the three lanes of traffic as he just flagged me down, opened the doors and they got in, Si visibly white and sweating in fear.

"He tried to fucking KILL ME!!" Si never swears, so he must've been spooked. I wasn't sure to laugh or not. I just waved sheepishly at all the drivers who had narrowly missed being involved in a multiple pile up.

"Home now, eh?" And he lit up a fag, placing the packet next to the sticker that said 'NO SMOKING'. All normal in Trevor land. We dropped him off, with a sigh of relief.

I never saw him again.

He died, from vascular dementia, after months of setting his flat alight, getting nicked for shoplifting, being found wandering round town in his pyjamas, being put in a secure home running and naked in the midnight corridors waving his cock at the nurses, and finally into Hospital, from where he never returned, and at the age of 98, he died. On Christmas Day. Christmas fucking day. Nice one.

Do I miss him? No. Was I upset? No, or, only for Gill, whom he had somehow managed, after *everything* he had done to her, to get her to be his skivvy for the last years of his life – so yes, sorry, only for her, as she was with him when he died and that can't be nice for anyone. I knew too that with the centre of power gone, Shelob, no longer at the centre of the web, holding us all in place with his poisonous threads, that the family would unravel, dissipate, no longer be in thrall. And so it proved – nobody sees anyone else now, has anything to share. We were all, essentially, different people, only connected by birth and once the ties that bound us were gone, so was the dynamic of family.

I have often looked back, from a distance of years, with wonder at Rod's family – all of them loving each other without condition which is what enabled them to thrive. Concern, the desire to protect and nourish each other were all sadly lacking in my family, and so despite the agonies caused by what happened with me and Rod, I would not change a single moment of it, as for those four years, I had a family, a family, all of whom loved and cherished me. That is irreplaceable in my heart and soul.

 My Dad died. I really didn't care.

Does it make me bad? I don't think so….. It makes me *honest*…..

And so, the Days of Summer drew to an end. Ferry tickets were booked, the car was packed; bizarrely Debs was away when we left so there no goodbyes to be said. We locked up and, Betty, with her axles nearly scraping the road, took us north, out of Cornwall….

A30…

M5…..

A35….

M27…

Southampton, Portsmouth, Brighton, Eastbourne, Hastings (fish and chips with our last English money), Folkestone, Dover…..

Bill Bryson once said:

"I can't think of anything that excites a greater sense of childlike wonder than to be in a country where you are ignorant of almost everything. Suddenly you are five years old again. You can't read anything, you have only the most rudimentary sense of how things work, you can't even reliably cross the street without endangering a life. Your whole existence becomes a series of interesting guesses."

My new life was about to begin. Finally.

CHAPTER THIRTEEN.

'THIS ABOVE ALL ELSE: TO THINE OWN SELF BE TRUE'.

In which our hero arrives in a new land, arrives in a safe place in his heart, arrives at the end of the search, meets more people than he knew existed who all think he's fab and plans to become Mr O'Corra-Bray. Or Bray-O'Corra. And, finally, at Journey's End, he walks into the sun.

'Dream Catch Me'.

by Newton Faulkner. No11. 1st September, 2007

I know who I am now! I can be anyone I wanna be!

~ ~ ~

Six months ago, almost to the day, I was living in a land of endless horizons with very little appearing on them, apart maybe from the same scene coming round again. Like a kind of zoetrope – same scenes, same people going past, doing the same things. I jumped off. As the Buddhists say: "JUMP! The net will appear!" I did. It did.

September 1st. Now, I am on a boat, watching the white cliffs of Dover, getting smaller, too small to see if there any bluebirds over them, watching England retreat, watching the great churns of the Channel spit and flick and glisten and thinking 'Oh my giddy aunt'. Or something similar. I just said that because as you now I don't swear. Unless it slips out. But that's another story…

On the ferry, bound for France.

There is a very strange pain in my heart. It seems cleft in twain. Half overbursting with joy and anticipation, the other full of anger and sadness at how I had been treated. By my Friends. You know, the ones who promised to love me forever, but haven't spoken to me or contacted me since April, 6 months now, since I met Simon.

These were the people with whom I shared weddings, funerals, birthdays and christenings. Deaths of mothers, fathers, sisters and pets. Sorrows and joys. Illness, fears and joyful recoveries. Seventeen years of intimacy with them all, and who have never, since the day I left for London with Simon, 'that bastard, who ate the food, drank the wine and took me as well'; since I met my 'whim' and had no idea what I was doing, but just fucked off, without a by your leave, with not a backward glance, spoken a single word to me.

Actually I did. Look back, I mean. Often, and with real sorrow. And as I gave up my homeland, my country, my language, my work and all of *YOU* to be where I knew my true love lay, I would have hoped that you, ONE Of you, might have asked how I was? You may not have agreed with what happened, but you could still have asked...."*Are you OK?*" That's just lazy, taking sides, and not the responsibility of treating us both equally. Just ask this: If it was all so perfect – why did I leave?

It's funny isn't it, the notion of 'break – up', how we all assume the 'left' is the only one suffering and the 'leaver' is having a whale of a time, with nary a care. Well, folks, it ain't so easy. In addition to the agony of separation, of giving up the security that long term relationships and friendships bring, there is a huge burden of guilt. Which is passed on to the new person who has to deal with all the strangeness of a new (if wished for) relationship and to cope with the feelings of terrible guilt of 'what I had done', no matter how blameless, no matter how dysfunctional it had been or how tired and exhausted the relationship was and it being absolutely the right time to go.

It mattered a lot at first. It mattered less and less as time went on. So, Jean, Mary, Richard, Rachel, Kath, Silu, Pauline, Tina, St.John, Chris, Derek, Alwyn, Louise, Judy, Colin, Jo, Pat, Edwin, Karl, Debbie, Mike, Audrey, Edwin, Roger et al.......I'm FINE!! Thanks for asking. Oh, wait! You didn't.

Still, the waters close over your head.....

We weren't done yet of course. I had a marriage certificate and house, both of which I no longer wanted. Back away from the Guilty Step.....it's the way of things. So, whilst still in Falmouth I had started the ball rolling and found a lovely solicitor who saw clearly and straight away that there was cause for separation on ground of 'unreasonable conduct'. I of course tried to keep saying "Oh it wasn't *THAT* bad", trying to assuage my guilt and feelings of failure, but as I told her more and more of my living situation over the years and all the complications arising from my diagnosis and the cancer - that - never- was debacle, it was becoming clearer to me that I had been suffering 'domestic abuse' for years and there were indeed, if I wanted, ground for divorce.

Was it ugly? No. Was it painful? A bit. But I had Si next to me every step of the way, every form, every meeting, supporting, upholding, never judging, always patient when I wasn't very nice, which was quite often, and understanding why.

I still had shed loads of stuff back at the house and once we'd moved, we were forever to and fro to Cornwall in our poor old Vera (Betty was scrapped as Si had written the poor old gal orf) and whilst Si wandered around the shops or stayed back in Falmouth I went back to the house to collect Stuff. Stuff which in reality, I neither needed nor wanted. It was truly weird seeing David – such little time had passed and I barely recognised him. It was like talking to a really prickly stranger. It WAS of course still my house, though he'd forbidden me to have a key (SEE? See what I mean?) I couldn't be fucked to argue anymore so it had to be 'by prior arrangement'...... MY house! MY stuff! Fucking cheek, but I was able to manage, as it was now just a numbers game: the stuff and the need to go grew less frequent and so the agro quotient fell too.

I'd go, we'd divvy up CDs (yep, really, just like in the films), he'd make me a sandwich, I'd sit on the workbench, just to make a point, he'd ask if I'd like "some of his crisps", I'd have a coffee, pack the car and drive away, over and over till there was nothing left. In all senses. In all ways.

Soon, it was all in France or down the dump.

During one of these times, I bore the brunt, and deservedly so, of Gaynor's anger and disappointment at me having lied to her. It was clear, given the car loads of stuff that was being extracted, I wasn't going 'for a few months'. So, shame faced and sad, I went in for a drink – David was away, so I slept in my house, that night, pissed as a pissed thing, just like the old days. Sort of. - and confessed. The whole story, including WHY I hadn't told her. She was just hurt, hurt and angry, and it was hard for her to have been shat on by, AND to be losing, her best friend, her buddy with whom she shared her heart, her dope and her wine. It was many months before we found peace again, where she had been made aware of just how duplicitous David could be, having nursed *his* heart fiercely after I'd 'deserted him', defended him and screamed at me. But, in *fermentum et veritas,* when the truth came out; when she DID realise how my hands had been tied, my voice silenced, her anger switched sides. Now she adores my man, has apologised twenty thousand times and all is well.

The divorce, amazingly, was uncontested. I don't know whether this was an admission of culpability (I doubt THAT somehow) or if he was just resigned to the fact that for once, he was unable to control what was to happen. I was surprised, and relieved, that he just accepted it – maybe he just took the line of least resistance…but in any event, he agreed and signed it off and hurrah! I was free.

And maybe, just maybe, there was a tacit acknowledgement that we simply weren't right for each other.

The house took longer; he was particularly obstructive, which ended up costing us a considerable amount of money as the market dropped, but I understand why – it was his home and he was probably angry / lost / scared at the prospect of being forced out. Also probably there was a huge amount of pissed offness as I was in charge of events – an alien landscape for him. Anyway, after much huffing and puffing we found a buyer, split the money and sailed off into our sunsets.

Except of course, we didn't. We were still linked - his Mum, dear Ruth who had promised to be my surrogate Mum and to whom I was close died so I was involved in that, at least emotionally. I held a little vigil and had a ceremony here in the garden for her. Well, for me, but you know what I mean. As for the multitude of Friends…..nothing. Not a call, not an email not a question, and it was this that obstructed my healing the most – I was unbelievably hurt by them, by this. *MY* friends – those that were pre-David or from Hungary or NODA Summer Schools were united and with one voice (but with varying amounts and swearing) asked *'How the fuck did you stay with him SO long?' 'He was a controller, a manipulator, a bully and you were well shot of him'*. How come I saw none of this? All those years….

I am not willing to say they were wasted; they weren't and we DID have some good times; we did lots and saw lots but it was not until I went to Hungary, after my reiki training, that I began to feel wrong, wrong in my **self** and in my heart – so how did it take five more years before I had the courage to leave? What would have happened if Simon hadn't appeared? If I hadn't done the website training? Started inviting strangers to our bed? This is all self-evident of course – all of those decisions, events, agreements (though usually not by me) all led to the point where I WOULD meet him, and by extension, leave. The Universe moves in mysterious ways. Reiki provides, if eyes are open to see and the heart open to receive.

I think now, hand on heart, that we really weren't very good for each other. Fuck knows how, or why, we stumbled on for so many years but as Baby Jesus or King James or somebody said:

'To everything there is a season, and a time to every purpose under the sun' and I guess things were going to take the time allotted until it became time to do something else. No fault, or fault on both sides. Just ran out of petrol. That's it.

And, DUH, here was the crux. Simon was not, is not, my Father. He is never judgemental, aggressive, belittling or controlling. And he is younger. Look back, you fool! Look back! In all the 'proper' (not necessarily successful or healthy) relationships I'd had, of any length anyway...everyone of 'em was older than me. Rod: +12; John: +23 (Shuddup, yes, really); David: +13. All in their way controllers, manipulators, bullies – and just like my Daddy. But they LOVED me, just like my Daddy didn't, but just like I wanted him to. How I didn't see this pattern before, fuck knows. Time after time. I just thought I fancied older blokes. When really, I was chasing the illusion that my Dad could like me, didn't mind I was a poof and was nice to me. Except, of course, really not one of them was. All of 'em just as destructive, just as ruinous to my self-esteem as he had been.

Until now. Until I met, was given, this wonderful man, 4 years my junior with no agenda, who loves me. Unconditionally. With no caveats, other than I love him back.

Lucky Mr. Lucky.

Slowly. Slowly, I adapted to my new life, supported gently, wisely by Simon, who never pushed, never rushed, letting go bit by bit and stepping, wide eyed, into a world where I was allowed an opinion, the answers to whose questions were valued; who was asked questions, where I was never belittled or made to feel inadequate...

...and with that sense of worth, the blood flowed back into my heart and into my penis as surely as the horrors of the previous months had prevented it. I have mentioned stiffies often during this diatribe and you, I bet, have thought 'is that all you think about?' Well, yes actually. But you have no idea how profound a gift it was to be able to be normal again, in all senses of the word, return to a world I had forgotten existed, and was finally blown apart at 11 a.am, on 11/11, 2004 and which I never thought it would ever be fixed.

Well Simon did. Sewed up the rents in my heart, soothed away the bruises. This is the last poem I wrote, not having needed to pour forth pain since we met, only joy.

The Healer

Gentle me, soothe my skin,

Erase the creases the day's bent in.

Unstitch me from the web;

Make me whole – not with plaster or daub,

But close subtly the rents in my heart;

Re-connect me to the lost pathways in which love lived in lives long lost.

Lie with me in astonished silent places,

Brushing off the slough of heavy duty and weighty care,

Till I am clean and open to you.

Then, into these newly cleansed wounds, pour the antiseptic of your love

To heal and suture my wounded pasts -

With high praise and low laughter,

With quick glance and slow caress,

While we join our subtle flesh and rock away our cares

Till we spill them each into the other's most secret places

And we lie, bathed in sweat and joy, seed and light

As we are welcomed home.

April, 2007.

Wedding Pic – the one and only!

In October 2010 we were married, well, PACSd, the French equivalent of a Civil Partnership and soon, thanks to that darling little M. Hollande, we'll marry and this time with a heart so open and eager because I know that this time it will be whole and pure and equal.

We went travelling, my man and I. We went back to Hungary, to Kesckemét, to Bosckai ut, the Tanítóképző Főiskolai, and stood outside my Office door in the *Angol nyelvi osztály,* the English Language Department, where I'd had an engraved plaque with my name; *'Nigel Bray, Angol tanár',* Teacher of English, in gold letters, where I had begun to heal; back to the minutiae of my life there.

Basic but mine....

He was fascinated, interested, full of admiration and praise – something I was still quite unused to – and it was amazing to me. We went to the wonders of Budapest, not to lay ghosts, but to see things with different eyes, and I felt a bit of pride to be showing him 'my city' and to do new things, to make new memories and reclaim it as my own, to share with HIM.

We went to Berlin too – it was awful, mostly, but I was able to show him wonders and make new memories and make it ours and for our honeymoon, the wonder of Barcelona were ours – new, unsullied and glorious.

Gaudi Park, Barcelona. Full of colour and joy.

Almost sixty years have passed since the start of this journey. 465 pages of stuff over the three volumes, 169,547 words. Years filled with more things than you can shake a stick at. Sorrows, and great joys. Amazing people and those who caused me harm. All necessary to give the tapestry its colours.

SO, dear kind and patient readers. All that remains then, is to look back see how it's looking on the old Lucky-ometer and take a reading....

Sure, there were really *really* bad things, - the vileness of my Father, his letters and insults and his actions and the terrible way he treated us and the resulting, lasting damage he did to us all; the terrible mess I made of people's hearts (and my own) as I was just a stupid man/child, unwise in the ways of love and how to treat people – you can trace this way way back to the first book – so I can only, rather late in the day, apologise. I was a twat. *Mea culpa*. My discovery that I had HIV (not very lucky there, eh?) and the terrible damage wrought to my body, my health and my self-esteem; I didn't treat you folks the way I should've and again, I apologise, for the lies I told to the people I loved – not necessarily my fault – but I acquiesced, nonetheless so I am equally to blame and responsible for the pain that weakness caused. *Mea culpa*; the sudden and devastating loss of my Mother and the effect that had on my behaviour as I was suddenly cast adrift; the loss of my wonderful Lager Blagger Extraordinaire, whose presence in my life was of immeasurable value, taken away from me and leaving me to fuck up alone; the enigma that was Rod – the pain he caused and the scars it left.

On the PLUS side, in the other pan – Oh most fortunate me! Contrarily, I was lucky to have had the Father I did, as it was a clear and constant warning to avoid ending up like him; Lucky to have had such a powerful force for good that was my Mother, who, with her unfailing faith in me and her Golden Ear Whizzes, even after death, kept me constant and determined to be the best I could, for her, in return for her loving me, come what may. Lucky to have been well educated and to have had a good and useful career, where I did good and good was done; Lucky to have had those years with Slobbidybobbidy, which though it ended badly, was joyous and full of hope; Lucky for the years I DID have Chris in my life and the fun and joy he brought me, the madness and the sorrow, worth it every bit; Lucky to have had the privilege of having lived in Hungary and be given the massive life lessons I learned there, and for that, I thank you - *köszönöm, Magyarország. Köszönöm szépen*; Lucky to have met Rod, as the joy he brought me, he and his family, far outweighs the mess that was the end. Lucky to have met David for he too, though times were good, was a lesson, in the end, in learning exactly the kind of man I wasn't and didn't want to be; Lucky to have had the special bond with Gill, who has loved me through it all and who is still here, and will be in France again soon where we will get bladdered and cry and tell tales and laugh as we always have; Lucky to have had Ann and Gaynor in my life too, the triumvirate of those Three Tall Women who all made me bigger, better and kinder and wiser and braver; Lucky to have been given the option in so many ways to express my creative side, at school, at College, with the many children and in Phoenix - we were *mahvellous* dahling, to do good things, to feed the flame; Lucky to have had Anna in my life who kept it real and true and I thank her for her love and wisdom in the very worst of times and of course, Lucky to have met Jim and been granted the gift of reiki and, for Michael who made it possible, eventually, to meet Simon, the love of what remains of my life and whose face I will see as the last breath leaves my body.

Meeting Simon, of course, was very lucky….but it wasn't luck.

Oh, and of course, you lot – for sticking with it to the very end – sharing my fears and joys, my loves and my secrets, my tales and adventures, my fuck ups and my successes – there have been many and often.

That's pretty fucking lucky, I'd say. Now I'll stop swearing. Maybe.

Hope it was worth the effort.

Peaces. Mr. Lucky. xxx

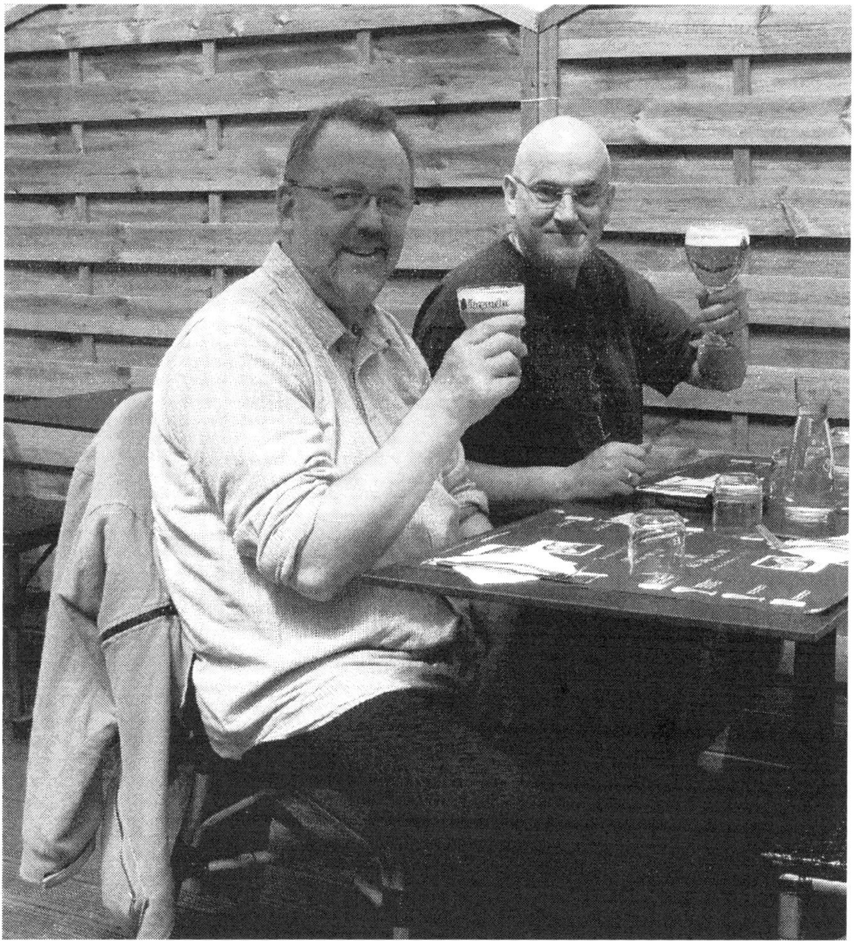

Printed in Great Britain
by Amazon.co.uk, Ltd.,
Marston Gate.